JUST ENOUGH TO MAKE A STORY

A *Sourcebook for Storytelling*

Third Edition

BY NANCY SCHIMMEL

SISTERS'
CHOICE
PRESS

1992

Copyright © 1978, 1982, 1992 by Nancy Schimmel
All rights reserved
Published in the United States by Sisters' Choice Books and Recordings, 1450 Sixth
Street, Berkeley, CA 94710. Single and bulk copies available by mail.
Third Edition, 1992

Quotation on page 40 from *The Lives of Children* by George Dennison. Copyright
© 1970, Random House, Inc. Used with the permission of Random House, Inc.

Quotation on page 39 from *The Joys of Yiddish* by Leo Rosten. Copyright © 1968,
McGraw-Hill Book Company. Used with the permission of McGraw-Hill Book
Company.

Quotation on page 10 from *Novel Experiences: Literature Units for Book Discussion
Groups in the Elementary School* by Christine Jenkins and Sally Freeman. Copyright ©
1990, Teacher Ideas Press, a division of Libraries Unlimited, P.O. Box 3988, Engle-
wood, CO 80155-3988. Used by permission.

Cataloging in publication data:

Schimmel, Nancy
    Just enough to make a story: A sourcebook for storytelling, by Nancy Schimmel.
    Third Edition.
    1. Storytelling   2. Women in folklore and mythology — Bibliography   3. Fairy
    tales — Bibliography   4. Ecology — Storytelling — Bibliography   I. Title
LB1042.S35   372.2'14
ISBN 0-932164-03-X

Design by Graphic Eye, Berkeley
Typesetting by Indian Rock Imagesetting, Berkeley
Printing by Mercuri Litho, El Cerrito

ACKNOWLEDGEMENTS

I would like to thank

my students, who taught me much that is in this book and with whom I worked out how to say it all

all the storytellers, particularly Connie Regan-Blake and Barbara Freeman whose FOLKTELLERS was a model for SISTERS' CHOICE, and Gay Ducey, my busy buddy

Elizabeth Sor, who taught me the paperfolds I used in "The Handsome Prince" and worked out the instructions for them

Irene Young, who took the photographs for the cover, and Tom Riles, who photographed me flying a goose girl at A Room of One's Own

all the anonymous quiltmakers, mostly women, whose artistry and imagination provided SISTERS' CHOICE with a name and logo, and Richard Dawkins, who worked out the Blind Watchmaker program as a demonstration of evolutionary processes, not as a tool for creating "computer embroideries" to decorate this book

Claudia Morrow, who found new books, typed, proofed and wrote some annotations, Sarah Satterlee and Karen Guma, eagle-eyed proofreaders, and Carole Leita, who read, reread, organized, criticized, proofed, indexed and blew bubbles

for my parents, who told me their stories
for Carole, who listens to mine

Tell Me a Story

words & music
© 1983 by Nancy Schimmel

Tell me a sto-ry, take me a-way, It's too soon to sleep and I'm too tired to play. When you were lit-tle, what did you do? Tell me a sto-ry that's all a-bout you.

Chorus: Tell me a story, take me away,
It's too soon to sleep and I'm too tired to play,
Verse: When you were little, what did you do?
Tell me a story that's all about you.

Find me a castle, find me a bird,
Find me a story that I've never heard.

I am a captain who sails on the sea,
Tell me a story that's all about me.

I'm gonna get cranky if you don't come soon,
Let's take a story and fly to the moon.

CONTENTS

ABOUT THE AUTHOR

Nancy Schimmel was born in Omaha but raised in California, where she still lives. Her midwestern father, William (Bud) Reynolds, told stories from his own experience to anyone who would listen, and since he was a good teller, they did. Nancy absorbed his economical, informal style. He was forty-two when she was born, so he already had a lot of stories about following the harvest as a young man, shipping out on a windjammer during the first World War, organizing the unemployed during the Depression. He worked as a union carpenter most of his life. Nancy's mother, Malvina Milder Reynolds, grew up in San Francisco and wrote her doctoral dissertation at UC Berkeley comparing a medieval French romance with folktales having a similar plot. She played fiddle in a dance band, did social work during the Depression, worked on an assembly line during World War II when Nancy was in elementary school (and wrote a newspaper column about it), ran her father's tailor shop after he died, and then started writing songs and singing them, introducing the songs with stories about how and why they were written. When Nancy was in her teens she watched her mother develop as a performer, and started her own love affair with the stage in high school and college dance programs. Nancy worked as a social worker, organized peace marches during the '60s, became a children's librarian, attended the third National Storytelling Festival at Jonesborough in 1975, and was inspired to break away and travel the country as a storyteller in a big white van called Moby Jane. In 1978 after teaching storytelling at the University of Wisconsin graduate library school, she wrote the first edition of *Just Enough to Make a Story*. She has since taught many classes and workshops and has brought her experience as teacher and teller into later editions of *Just Enough*. She has become a songwriter herself, and her cassette of ecology songs for children, *All In This Together*, won a 1990 Parent's Choice Gold Award. She is beginning to tell family stories as well as folk and original stories, and to write stories she doesn't plan to tell.

PREFACE TO THE THIRD EDITION

I first published this book in 1978. I have updated the bibliographies every time I reprinted it, and changed it substantially enough in 1982 to warrant calling that a second edition. When I read over the 1987 reprinting in 1990 I could see that it was time again for deeper changes than just adding to the lists. I am more certain of some things than I was in 1978, and less certain of others. In the world of professional storytelling, issues like copyrights and credits are being discussed and must at least be mentioned. Issues in the larger world are acknowledged in the new list of "Ecology Stories and Songs" and additions to the "Stories in Service to Peace" list.

To make room for the new and still keep the book "just enough" I have pared away some of the old. "Barney McCabe" is gone, because Guy and Candie Carawan's *Ain't You Got a Right to the Tree of Life? The people of John's Island, South Carolina—their faces, their words, and their songs* is back in print in a revised and expanded edition (University of Geor-gia Press, 1989). The book includes several other stories besides "Barney McCabe" and, more importantly, contains background information on the culture from which the stories come. Also, some older out-of-print books have been removed from the "Active Heroines" and "Sources for Stories to Tell to Adults" lists. If you have an earlier edition of *Just Enough* and access to a historical collection, you may want to keep a copy of the old "Active Heroines."

Most of the increase in price in this new edition is due to an increase in basic costs, but a small amount is to offset some part of the impact of the book's production on the environment: using part-recycled paper for the text and sending a donation to the Green Belt Movement, a women-run tree-planting program in Kenya. (If you wish to donate also, send checks or money orders, not cash, to Green Belt Movement, Moi Avenue, P.O.Box 67545, Nairobi, Kenya. Individual trees can be sponsored for $10.)

INTRODUCTION: THE TAILOR

IN A VILLAGE ONCE LIVED a poor tailor. He had made overcoats for many people, but he had never made one for himself, though an overcoat was the one thing he wanted. He never had enough money to buy material and set it aside for himself, without making something to sell. But he saved and saved, bit by bit, and at last he had saved enough. He bought the cloth and cut it carefully, so as not to waste any. He sewed up the coat, and it fit him perfectly. He was proud of that coat. He wore it whenever it was the least bit cold. He wore it until it was all worn out.

At least he thought it was all worn out, but then he looked closely and he could see that there was just enough good material left to make a jacket. So he cut up the coat and made a jacket. It fit just as well as the coat had, and he could wear it even more often. He wore it until it was all worn out.

At least he thought it was all worn out, but he looked again, and he could see that there was still enough good material to make a vest. So he cut up the jacket and sewed up a vest. He tried it on. He looked most distinguished in that vest. He wore it every single day. He wore it until it was all worn out.

At least he thought it was all worn out, but when he looked it over carefully, he saw some places here and there that were not worn. So he cut them out, sewed them together, and made a cap. He tried it on, and it looked just right. He wore that cap outdoors and in, until it was all worn out.

At least it seemed to be all worn out, but when he looked, he could see that there was just enough left to make a button. So he cut up the cap and made a button. It was a good button. He wore it every day, until it was all worn out.

At least he thought it was all worn out, but when he looked closely, he could see that there was just enough left of that button to make a story, so he made a story out of it and I just told it to you.

Now I didn't make that story out of a button, but I did make it out of a song. A long time ago, I heard someone sing a Yiddish folk song at a concert and explain in English what the song said, which was the same as the story except that the person in the song made a song instead of a story out of the button.* I didn't remember the song, but I liked the idea, and years later I tried it out as a story, first on a first grade class and later at a convalescent hospital.

I was working at a library just a block from the hospital. I told stories once a month at the hospital, and each time, after I did my stories and songs, we would sit around at tables and have tea and cookies. About the third time I went there, I told "The Tailor." Afterwards, I sat at a table with a man and a woman. The woman said, "You know, it's funny you told the story about a tailor today, because my father was a tailor. He was in Germany and he wanted to come to this country but he didn't have enough money, so he stowed away. When the ship had gotten out to sea, he poked his nose out of his hiding place and went out to see if it was safe. He overheard someone saying they were looking for a tailor, so he went right back to his hiding place and stayed there. At the end of the trip, he found out that they were just looking for a tailor to do some tailoring, they weren't looking for a stowaway at all, and he had missed out on a job."

---

*The song, in English, is available on *Songs of the Holidays* sung by Gene Bluestein on Folkways FC 7554. It is called "I Had a Little Coat."

I said, "That's funny that you're telling me this story about your father who was a tailor, because my grandfather was a tailor. His family scraped up enough money to send him to this country, but he didn't like it. He had been a tailor's apprentice in Budapest, but in New York he was working in a sweatshop, and the streets weren't paved with gold after all, and he was homesick. He was living with his uncle, but it wasn't home. On the Sabbath, on Saturdays, he would go down to the docks and look wistfully at the ships and think about Budapest. One day a man who spoke Yiddish came up to him and asked why he looked so sad. He said he was wishing he could go home on one of these ships, but he didn't have the money. The man said, 'Well, I can take care of you. You just sign on as part of the crew, and work your way across. When you get to the Old Country, you jump ship and find your way home. And since I speak English and you don't, I can get you on a ship going in the right direction.' My grandfather thought that was a fine idea, and he followed the man into an office, and he signed his name here, and he signed his name there, and he was in the U. S. Navy for four years.

"Luckily, he liked the Navy, so much so that he re-enlisted twice, and at the end of his service he became a naval tailor, which he was until the day he died. And since he was on a ship with a crew of New York Irish, this Jewish tailor from Budapest spoke English with a bit of an Irish brogue all his life."

After the woman and I had this little exchange, the man, who had been just sitting there not saying a word, said "What did you say the tailor made out of the button?"

"A story."

He said, "What?"

I said, "A story. Out of the button he made the story I told you."

"Oh!" he said, "I thought you said buttonhole."

The man had a pretty good story there. Not the story I told, but one that makes sense, because after the button wears out you've got nothing left, and what do you make out of nothing? You make a hole. And what kind of a hole does a tailor make? A buttonhole.

And indeed this is the way stories and songs change. A word goes through a change of time or place, or through a hearing aid, and comes out nonsense. The listener, who becomes the next teller, changes the word so it makes sense again. And I, not remembering that the Yiddish folk song was in first person, made the protagonist a tailor, because that made sense to this granddaughter of a tailor.

We all have stories: stories that are handed down in our families, stories and jokes that we hear and retell with small changes, and stories about things that happen to us, like the story I just told about the time I went to the convalescent hospital in Belmont. Some of us are professional storytellers, some of us are amateurs, some tell out of choice and some out of necessity, but we are all storytellers, even if the only stories we tell are stories about why we were late to work this morning.

We are all storytellers, but some of us tell stories better, some of us tell better stories, and some of us are better at remembering the right story for the right moment. The skills of choosing, learning and telling stories can be acquired, and I have tried to pass on some of what I know about them in this book. I believe one can also acquire some of the attitudes that help make a good storyteller. By reading about folklore and by reading and hearing and telling many tales, one learns to respect the story, making it one's own without completely wrenching it from its tradition or meaning, or changing a special flavor it might have.

The stories I have included in this book change every time I tell them, every time anyone tells them. But sometimes people can't remember enough of a story I've told to be able to tell it at all, and they ask me, "Is this story written down?" So here they are, locked inside this book. It is up to you to release them.*

---

*Please feel free to tell to a live audience, face to face, any of the stories printed herein, but do mention your source. To reprint, record or broadcast the story, you will need to ask for permission.

CHOOSING A STORY

AT THE END OF A storytelling course, one of my students said, "I was disappointed at first that you didn't just tell us how to tell stories; then I realized that you couldn't." And indeed I cannot. I can tell you how *I* find, learn and tell stories, and what works for other storytellers I know. You can pick out what works for you.

People tell stories successfully so many ways that I can't find any hard and fast rules. Well, one. Tell stories you like to tell. And this rule has two sides to it. One is enjoying the story itself for whatever reason — the plot, the language, the associations it has for you. The other is enjoying the telling of it, which depends somewhat on the effect the story has on the audience — an effect you can't always predict when you choose the story.

I have to read, and hear, and sift through many stories to find one I want to make the effort to learn and tell. When I hear a story told, even badly told, I can judge it better than when I read it. If I read a story I think I like well enough, I read it aloud to myself, a friend or a tape recorder, usually all three, before I decide.

A good story to tell can have complex language but it should have a fairly simple plot, without subplots and digressions — unless digressions are the point of the story, as in Mark Twain's "The Notorious Jumping Frog of Calaveras County." The main action should begin fairly quickly, without too much introduction. It helps if the plot comes to a satisfying conclusion, so the listeners know the story is over. A formula ending like "Snip, snap, snout, this tale's told out" can also signal the story's end. If the ending isn't obvious, try pausing before the last sentence and then saying it slowly.

If I am telling a story from my own experience, I try to apply some of the same criteria — sorting out the important from the unimportant details, making sure the introduction (why I was where it hap-

pened, who the other characters were) doesn't outweigh the action. (*It is a foolish thing to make a long prologue, and to be short in the story itself. 2 Maccabees. II, 32*)

If I like the point or the plot of a story but not the telling, I look for another version before I decide to cut or change the story myself. For instance, I liked the plot of "The Peddler of Ballaghadereen" (*Way of the Storyteller*), and the language was fine, but the introduction seemed to go on and on about the goodness of the peddler — which was not what drew me to the story. So I went to "The Pedlar of Swaffham" (*More English Fairy Tales*) and found a briefer telling in which the part about belief in dreams had relatively more importance. If you do want to cut or rework a story, it will still be helpful to look at different versions, if you can find them. You will see what variations are possible while still keeping the essentials. Both Colwell and DeWit (listed on page 13) discuss how to cut and expand stories. In some stories, it is the language itself, and the mood it sets, that I feel are most important, not the plot. Learning these stories word for word is more difficult for me than learning a plot and telling it in my own words, but it is very satisfying.

Language can help make a story easier to learn. Verse is easier to memorize than prose, and recurring rhymes or rhythmic phrases in a story give both teller and listener something familiar to hang on to. Most stories in easy-to-learn forms — cumulative tales like "The Old Woman and Her Pig," stories with repetition of rhymes and phrases like "The Three Billy Goats Gruff" — are nursery tales best told to children under eight. But there are some that can be told to older children and adults. "The Tailor" is one that works for all ages, "Lazy Jack" for older as well as younger children, "The Yellow Ribbon" (*Juba This and Juba That*) for older children. "Mr. Fox" is an easy-to-learn story that I tell to adults and teens rather than to children.

If the language of a story does not make it easy to learn, a very logical, sequential plot may help. In "The Little Red Hen," for instance, the wheat must be planted before it is cut, threshed before it is milled and so on, whereas the mishaps that befall "The Husband Who Was to Mind the House" (*Womenfolk and Fairy Tales* by Rosemary Minard) could conceivably happen in some other sequence, so they don't order themselves in the memory without some effort.

A shorter story is usually easier to learn, but not always. "The King o' the Cats" is about half as long as "Lazy Jack," but I found it more difficult to learn and tell. It is a story within a story, and I found I had to stick more closely to the exact wording or get mixed up.

I was more often called upon to tell a particular type of story or a story on a particular subject when I was a librarian than I am now, but it still happens. If I have a story in mind that I like, and enough time, I can use the request to make myself work on a story I had been putting off learning. But if I don't have a story in mind, I don't make promises, lest I put myself in the position of learning a story I don't like. As a librarian, I could read aloud a story that was all right but not near enough to my heart to learn. (Preparing to read a story aloud is the same as the beginning of learning a story — reading it aloud and thinking about it, maybe recording it and listening again.) Now I may find or write a song that fits the request, but more often I find an aspect of a story that I already know but hadn't seen in just this way before. I may bring that aspect out in the introduction or in comments after the story, or context may make the connection for the audience.

While it's a good idea to tell only stories you like, it is possible to find a kind of story you like and feel safe with, and not try other kinds — to tell only funny stories, or fairy tales, or whatever your preference is. Not that you should feel bad about neglecting a kind you don't like after you've given it a fair try. I didn't tell any Greek myths until I read Jean Shinoda Bolen's *Goddesses in Everywoman: A New Psychology of Women* (Harper, 1984) and I still only tell a couple.

You may read dozens of stories for each one you learn. It's a good idea to list these somewhere — copying title pages from story collections and making notes on them is an easy way — so that later, when someone asks you for a story about guinea pigs, or whatever, you won't go crazy trying to remember where you saw one.

Many of the stories I tell come from Joseph Jacobs' two volumes of *English Fairy Tales*. Many tellers I know also find these stories easy and satisfying to learn and tell but others have their own favorites. I also tell several stories from *The Magic Orange Tree* and *Womenfolk and Fairy Tales,* and many stories I have not found in books but have heard or lived.

I've listed here some books that contain good stories to start on. The children's librarian at your nearest library can help you find others to tell to children and adults, and the library probably has *Storyteller's Sourcebook...A Subject, Title, and Motif Index to Folklore Collections for Children* edited by Margaret Read MacDonald (Gale, 1982), which will help you find stories on particular subjects or from specific cultures. A smaller but more recent index to stories (including non-traditional ones) is *Stories—A List of Stories to Tell and Read Aloud,* eighth edition (New York Public Library, 1990).

Story Collections

Some of the collections listed below are out of print. Libraries often save last copies of out-of print story collections for librarians and storytellers to use in the library. Another source is A. Craighead, 5368 Wonder Drive, Fort Worth, TX, 76133-1927, a dealer in used books for storytelling. *Children Tell Stories* not only contains twenty-five easy-to-tell stories but also indexes many more on pages 158 to 166.

Arbuthnot, May Hill. *The Arbuthnot Anthology of Children's Literature.* Scott, Foresman, 1976 (o.p.).

Caduto, Michael J., and Joseph Bruchac. *Keepers of the Earth: Native American Stories and Environmental Activities for Children.* Fulcrum, 1988.

Courlander, Harold, and George Herzog. *The Cow–Tail Switch and Other West African Stories.* Holt, 1988 (c. 1949). Plus his other collections from Africa, Asia, Haiti and North America.

The Diane Goode Book of American Folk Tales and Songs. Dutton, 1989. [Compiled by Ann Durell.]

Contains an African American version of "Talk" that is simpler than the African version.

Ginsburg, Mirra. *Three Holes and One Doughnut: Fables from Russia.* Dial, 1970, o.p. Very short stories.

Hamilton, Martha, and Mitch Weiss. *Children Tell Stories: A teaching guide.* Richard C. Owen, 1990. [135 Katonah Ave., Katonah, NY 10536.] Includes over 25 short, easy stories.

Hamilton, Virginia. *The People Could Fly: American Black Folktales.* Knopf, 1985.

Jacobs, Joseph. *English Fairy Tales.* Dover, 1967 (c.1898). Plus his other collections from the British Isles.

Lester, Julius. *The Knee–High Man and Other Tales.* Dial, 1972. Short, tellable stories from the African American tradition.

MacDonald, Margaret Read. *Look Back and See: Twenty Lively Tales for Gentle Tellers.* H. W. Wilson, 1991. Includes notes on telling each tale and on the tales' origins and variants.

MacDonald, Margaret Read. *Twenty Tellable Tales: Audience Participation Folktales for the Beginning Storyteller.* Wilson, 1986. These easy stories can be done with or without participation.

Minard, Rosemary. *Womenfolk and Fairy Tales.* Houghton, 1975.

Rockwell, Anne. *The Three Bears and 15 Other Stories.* Crowell, 1975.

Tashjian, Virginia. *Juba This and Juba That: Story Hour Stretches for Large and Small Groups.* Little, 1969.

Tashjian, Virginia. *With a Deep Sea Smile: Story Hour Stretches,* Little, 1974.

Wolkstein, Diane. *The Magic Orange Tree and Other Haitian Folktales.* Knopf, 1978.

Yep, Laurence. *The Rainbow People.* Harper, 1989. Folktales collected in the 1930's in California from Chinese immigrants and retold recently by a fine writer.

Yolen, Jane. *Favorite Folktales from Around the World.* Pantheon, 1986.

LEARNING A STORY

THE ONLY RULE I KNOW for learning a story is this: learn the plot first, then learn the words if you want to. If you learn the words only, and forget one, you might get stuck; but if you know the sequence of events, and forget a word, you can fake it till you pick up the thread of the words again.

People have different methods of learning plots. Some visualize the events, scenes, characters. They run this movie over inside their heads until the sequence is fixed, then describe it out loud in their own words or learn the subtitles already written by the author or reteller. I don't visualize easily; my connection with a story is more kinesthetic and emotional. I know how a character moves and when she has a sinking feeling in the pit of her stomach but not what she is wearing or what color her hair is. I usually learn a story more by logic— trying to reconstruct the sequence in my mind, realizing that this incident can't happen until that one has. This way I get the events organized, then I try to do the same thing aloud. I must use words to think through the plot, and I may then have to unlearn them if I decide to use the author's or reteller's words. Visualizing is probably the better method, but not the only one. One way to help yourself visualize a story is to draw a map of the action. You can also walk through a scene, imagining where the other characters are, trying out posture and movements that you might not use in performance, but that will help you get to know your characters. You don't have to say everything you know about the scene, characters and events of your story, but the more you know the more convincing your telling will be.

If you are telling personal stories, your problem is not learning the story but recalling it. Visualizing can help here too. Donald Davis suggests exploring a house you used to live in by mentally walking through it and noting the look, sound and smell of each room. Often this will evoke memories of events that took place in those rooms.

If you are a beginner, you can make learning your first few stories easier by starting with something familiar, either an easy favorite from your own childhood or a book you have read aloud many times. I had read *Caps for Sale* over and over at library storytimes, but didn't know I could tell it without the book until it was requested at a neighborhood art fair and I didn't have the book with me. I tried it anyway, and surprised myself. I have never used the book since.

Once I have learned the plot, I usually read the story aloud several more times, or listen to it on the tape recorder (a good method to use while driving). I run the story through in my head, trying out the words. As I do this, I think about how to tell it. Why did this character say what she said? What was she thinking? How did she feel? What was she trying to convey to the other character? (Ideally, I do this each time I perform the story, too, to review it and also to come up with fresh approaches to it.)

I sometimes memorize the first paragraph or two (for a smooth start), any rhymed or repeated phrases, and probably the ending, especially if it is a formula ending. By this time I am familiar enough with the words to know whether I like them so well that I want to memorize them all, whether I prefer the words I found in learning the plot, or whether (as is often the case) I want to try for something in between—getting closer to the written words without memorizing, which means more checking back to the original as I work, but not working from it.

As to whether memorizing or telling in one's own words is more traditional, that depends on the tradition. An Inuit storyteller is corrected if the story is not told exactly the same each time, while Zunis prefer a teller who embroiders on the basic plot. In the Anglo-American tradition, the tale tends to be a free-phrase form, meaning that the words are subject to change, in contrast to proverbs and charms, which are fixed-phrase. If a riddle or proverb appears in a story, it will not change much, even though the rest of the story is retold in entirely different words. Ballads and other stories told in rhyme are fixed-phrase throughout. While they are easier to memorize, there is much less freedom, within the rhyme and rhythm, to fake it if you forget a word or two.

Usually I decide to use the author's words if the story is not a folktale, or if a folktale is retold so well that any change seems to weaken it (this is rare). Sometimes, however, the plot itself hinges on the exact wording of the dialogue, as in "Clever Manka" or "Ticoumba and the President." Then parts of the dialogue at least must be memorized. I also try to remember turns of phrase that seem to characterize a region or culture or a particular story. In "Barney McCabe," for instance, I keep "That ain't nothing but your grandma frock-tail switchin' to get your supper hot," but I substitute "master" for "maussa." Unless a teller has lived in the region, it is difficult to reproduce dialect naturally and correctly, without overdoing it. It is impossible to do so from the written word, as you can tell by reading "Barney McCabe" in *Ain't You Got a Right to the Tree of Life* and then listening to it told on *Moving Star Hall Singers* by the same person from whom it was collected for the book.

As for the accents people new to the language lend English from their native tongue, these can only be heard when they speak English. If two speakers of Spanish, for instance, are talking to each other, they speak in *unaccented* Spanish. I have heard non-Spanish-speaking tellers use Spanish-accented English to recount a story from Spain, but I believe the true translation of unaccented Spanish (or whatever language) is unaccented English. That is what I use to recount a conversation between two people speaking their own language, and to narrate a story taking place in a non-English-speaking country.

Sometimes very slight changes can make a story more comfortable to tell. Courlander's retellings, for instance, are simple, with short sentences. Even in parts you might memorize, you may find yourself running sentences together with "and" so they will sound more like spoken language. In Carl Sandburg's "Kiss Me" I have replaced "the men who change the alphabets" with "the people who change the alphabets," which is more comfortable for me to use, yet it doesn't sound out of place. I didn't like the elephant eating people in "Unanana and the Elephant" (*Womenfolk and Fairy Tales*) until I heard Sandra MacLees have the animals say "Oh, *that* elephant," implying that elephants don't normally do such things.

When I think I have learned the story, I try telling it while doing something else—dishes, driving—so that I will get to know it well enough to overcome the distraction of seeing the audience. Different tellers use different distractions—telling to a mirror, telling with the radio on, telling to family, friends, neighbors, car pool. Either a live audience or a tape recorder can catch words or phrases that are not clearly enunciated; a live audience can also catch places where meaning isn't clear. If the story uses an unfamiliar word, and that word is vital to the understanding of the plot, I try to use a more familiar synonym in another sentence rather than sticking it in right after the unfamiliar word as a definition, which can sound stilted. Occasionally I will slip in a definition as I introduce the story. I don't like to replace the unfamiliar word entirely, as some of the fun of storytelling is enjoying the richness of the language.

At this point I am through with what is for me the bad part, learning the story; and I can get on to one of the better parts, learning to *tell* the story.

TELLING A STORY

AS I LEARN THE STORY I am thinking about how to tell it, but at this point I can really start playing with it. What do I want to emphasize about the story? Is it quiet, funny, scary? Can I make it more or less scary depending on how I tell it? Would I like to give the story special treatment…gestures the audience can follow in *Caps for Sale?* different voices for different characters in "The Three Bears"? a quiet, dreamlike telling for "Umai"?

Starting a story at a walking pace will give room to speed up when the action gets exciting or to slow down for suspense or emphasis. Probably the most common mistake is to tell too fast. This can be caused by nervousness or by lack of faith in the story or the listeners — a feeling that "most people have heard this or won't be interested so I can just get it over with quickly." If the teller believes in the story and gives it its due, even listeners who have heard the story will enjoy it again.

On the other hand, speaking too slowly, particularly drawing out a long word, can sound condescending — as though you don't think the audience can keep up with you. Listen to Carl Sandburg telling *Rootabaga Stories* (Caedmon) to find out how slowly a teller can speak and get away with it.

Along with pace, pauses are important in setting off one part of the story from another. A pause can mark the transition between the introductory description ("Once upon a time…") and the beginning of the action ("So one day…"). Short pauses can set off a piece of dialogue from the "he said" or from the next speaker's line. A longer pause can build suspense. A pause before the last line can set the audience up for the ending.

If a pause is too long, people might wonder if you have forgotten the next line. However, if you do need to search for a word, it is better to pause for a bit than to fill in with "uh" or with an apology. If you forget or make a mistake, just correct it with-out apology, as you do in everyday conversation. We are all used to people making mistakes when they talk, and we can even figure out what people really meant to say when they make a slip they don't hear or don't think is important enough to correct. A sure tipoff to a memorized story is a teller correcting a "mistake" with another word that means the same thing.

If you realize halfway through the story that you left out something important earlier on, put it in as casually as possible, keeping the tone and rhythm of the story. "Now, everyone knew that…" or "He recollected that…" or even "Now, I should have told you that…" but not "Uh oh! I forgot to tell you about the…" Experienced tellers don't stop making mistakes — they just learn how to repair them with-out fuss. Also, pros don't apologize *before* they tell a story.

Loudness can be used for emphasis at times, rather than pace or pauses, but it must be used carefully. A small difference in volume will be quite notice-able, especially in a small room or a quiet story. A large increase can jolt your audience more than you meant to, while a large decrease can make the back row miss just the line you meant to emphasize. Again, a moderate volume to begin with will give scope for variation either way. At first you will have to enlist the help of your listeners to let you know whether you can be heard. With large audiences it is always good to check this, as there may be out-side noises you are unaware of which are bother-ing the last few rows. On the other hand, sustained loud telling can make an audience jumpy.

Whether or not you use gestures, and if so, how much, depends on how comfortable they feel to you. This, in turn, depends on how much you use them in conversation and how appropriate they seem to a particular story. I use lots of gestures in a straightforward story like *Caps for Sale* or "Lazy

Jack" but hardly any when I tell a story rich in imagery like "Umai" or "Fiddler, Play Fast, Play Faster." And "lots" doesn't mean every possible gesture. Fast gestures may be used to help define a character, but are distracting if used throughout a story. The words tell the story; the gestures add emphasis and can also help define an unfamiliar word. When I am learning and telling a story, I try to notice which gestures work. However, when I review a story I have already learned, I review the words but don't rehearse the gestures. I want the gestures to grow out of the words as I tell the story.

A video or audio tape or, better yet, a live storyteller is worth a thousand (written) words on the subject of gestures and voices in storytelling. For an excellent demonstration of the use of different voices listen to Johnny Moses tell "Basket Lady" or "The Slow Talking Man" on *Traditional Stories of the Northwest Coast* (tape available from The Red Cedar Circle, P. O. Box 1210, La Conner, WA 98257). I use different voices much less often than gestures; they come less naturally to me, and it's hard to remember to be consistent in giving each character a different accent or pitch unless the story itself reminds you, as "The Three Bears" does. Not using defined voices doesn't mean that characters all sound alike. They may be conveying quite different emotions, but I can express those emotions in my own voice, as I would if I were feeling them myself. Tellers vary as to how much emotion they put into their voices when they tell. I also vary the amount depending on the story. Tall tales, for instance, can be told pretty deadpan. Certainly, when I listen to a tall tale, I don't like to hear the teller sound astonished. I want the audience reaction left to the audience.

Likewise, when I am the listener, I want to make my own judgment about the story or book that is being presented, and not have the teller usurp my role by breaking into the story line to remark "Isn't this a beautiful picture?" or by saying "Wasn't that a nice story?" at the end. I always resented fiercely the questions at the end of each chapter in school readers, so now I prefer not to ask questions at the end of the telling. I often encourage the audience to ask questions, and sometimes turn to the audience to get an answer to an audience question.

It is natural for a teller to want immediate feedback on the performance and choice of story, but people don't always know immediately how they feel about an event, and can't always put their feelings into words when they do know. If you tell stories to the same group over a period of time, you find out that a child may stare out the window during the whole program and then go home and recite every story to a parent, or act out a favorite story in solitary play. But if you are telling to audiences that you won't see again, please take my assurance that this is so.

Some tellers like to discuss stories with children afterwards to help them process the story and to offer time for reflection before the next story or activity. In general, I think the only questions worth asking are the ones with no right answers.

Christine Jenkins and Sally Freeman are talking about book discussion in their guide, *Novel Experiences* (Teacher Ideas Press, 1990), but they use questions about a folktale to exemplify the kind of queries that promote thought rather than short-circuiting it. "In book discussion groups, students do not merely answer recall questions — they work together to discern the meaning of the text and, in doing so, develop higher-level comprehension skills. Many children enjoy talking about what they have read but have a hard time getting beyond 'I liked the part where…' and 'I didn't like the part where…'

"Good discussion questions are specific to the story. For example, instead of asking, 'What kind of character is Goldilocks?' the leader might ask group members, 'Why do you think Goldilocks always chose the biggest chair and bowl and bed first?' The leader then asks students to support their answers with examples from the text. Good discussion questions are more than factual recall questions and should encourage a variety of responses based upon each group member's interpretation of the story. The leader is there to facilitate the discussion by keeping it focused on the text at hand."

What comes before the story needs to be thought out as well. I would rather say "This is a story from…" than "This is a story about…" because a story can be about different things to different people, and I don't want to narrow the possibilities. In the last list in this book, Sisters' Choices, I talk about how I introduce "The Foolish Frog," "The King o' the Cats" and "The Man Who Walked on Water." I also talk about what I do *after* I tell "Barney McCabe."

There is no rule that says a teller must meet the eye of each listener during the course of a story, but if you look mostly at the floor or ceiling, the audience could get the idea that you are afraid of them or not interested in them. If you are telling for the first time, and are convinced that looking people in the eye will make you forget the entire story, look *just* over their heads. I look around at different faces, because I feel that looking at just a few people puts a burden on them to look interested. Of course my eye is drawn back most often to those faces that do look most interested, but with children it is prudent to give some attention to the restless ones, because it may keep them from getting so wriggly that they bother their neighbors.

I heard Ray Hicks, a North Carolina farmer and wildcrafter who is also a fine storyteller, tell a Jack tale to an audience of about three hundred at an early National Storytelling Festival in Jonesborough. Like most traditional tellers, he was probably used to telling to twenty-five people or less. What he did was to maintain eye contact with about twenty-five people in the front center of the audience, while the rest of us, instead of having a story told to us, watched him tell the story to that group, watched them react to it, and saw him enjoy their reactions. It worked.

A little nervousness is not a bad thing. It keeps me on my toes, alert to the audience and listening to the story, so I don't lose my place. The trick is to not show the nervousness. The problem is that you don't always know how you show it. I didn't know how I showed mine until I saw a video of myself — I lick my lips. A video (or your best friend) can tell you what you do — twist your feet, wring your hands, say "uh" at the beginning of each phrase, clear your throat (bad for your voice!), brush the hair out of your eyes. Once you are aware of your habit, you can work on breaking it (or get a haircut). To work on the nervousness itself, if you have more

than a little, read Eloise Ristad's excellent chapter on the subject, "Clammy Hands and Shaky Knees," in her book *A Soprano on Her Head* (Real People Press, 1982). She works with musicians and singers, but her method will be helpful to any performer. Here's a tip from my voice teacher: if nervousness makes your mouth dry, clenching your teeth a couple of times may fool your saliva glands into thinking you are eating and they will start to work again. Also remember to breathe: stage fright is excitement without breathing.

I don't always enjoy a story the first time I tell it to an audience. This may mean it's not a good story for me, but it is more likely that I am just not used to telling it yet, or that I have not found the right audience, or the right introduction, or the right way (for me) of telling it. I need many tellings to become really comfortable with some stories. I also depend on audience reaction and my feelings as I tell a story to let me know if I should cut it or extend it, ham it up or tell it straight. And the better I know a story, the more attention I can pay to the audience — so this is a long, spiral process. I am still learning to tell stories I have told for years.

By choosing well and telling stories over and over, I have enough confidence in each story and in the process so that I don't need to dress a story up with unnecessary dramatics or props. "Unnecessary" is, of course, a matter of taste, but *prop* is short for *property* and should not be expected to hold the teller upright. A student in one of my classes said she had read somewhere about "having the patience to do something badly" and this is certainly necessary in practicing and beginning to tell a story. So don't lose heart — it gets better.

When I am first telling a story, it usually changes a fair amount at each telling, then after a while it settles down and only changes slightly. If you hear me tell the same story many times at its settled stage, you may think I memorized it. But if you check back to my source, you will find that the wording is quite different. Other tellers say they have the same experience. To refresh my feeling about a story I've told too often, I will sometimes sing the entire thing operatic *recitativo* style. (I only do this in the privacy of my own vehicle.)

Someone said of a certain writer of young adult novels that she wrote dialogue not the way teenagers talk, but the way they like to think they talk. And when I tell a story, I usually try to sound not like somebody else, but like me at my best, without the *uhs* and *you knows* that spatter everyday conversation, and without the bright cheerfulness that comes over even the most sensible people when they talk to the very young. Of course, if you want to present a folktale as something that happened to you, as many tellers do, then you will want to leave more "everydayness" in your speech to make it sound more convincing.

I have given you my ideas on how to tell a story. The decision on how *you* will tell any story is, finally, a matter of taste, of personal style, of experience and of being aware of your listeners — that you neither bore them with monotone voice, nor embarrass them with overacting, nor overshadow their response to the story with your own.

Knowledge of your material can help you make decisions about performing it. I have listed some readings about folklore as well as storytelling at the end of this chapter. Talking to members of the culture from which the story comes (or reading about that culture) is always helpful. The less I know about a culture, the more reluctant I am to change anything in a story. For instance, I ad lib a lot when I do *It Could Always Be Worse,* but when I do it in tandem, I have to remind non-Jewish partners not to have the rabbi suggest that the man bring a pig into the house. Even in an exaggerated story, that would be asking too much.

When you tell a story that is not your own, mentioning your source is the courteous thing to do, whether that source is an author, a reteller, another performer or your next-door neighbor. I think there is also such a thing as courtesy to a culture. If you get a story from a book that is called *Winter-Telling Stories* because the Kiowa tell them only in winter, think about whether you want to tell those stories in spring, summer or fall. If you decide to tell them

anyway, you can explain that you are acting outside that tradition. The *Yarnspinner* (NAPPS newsletter), December 1990, has a series of articles on researching tales from cultures other than your own. "Recognizing and Acknowledging the Contexts of Story" in Anne Pellowski's *The World Of Storytelling* (Expanded and Revised Edition, Wilson, 1990, pp. 227-229) also addresses this issue.

If you get a story from a copyrighted book or recording, more than courtesy is involved. If you are a teacher or librarian telling in your own school or library, your educational use of that story comes under the "fair use" doctrine, and you need not worry about copyright law. But when people pay to hear you tell, or when you wish to record stories, you must pay attention to copyright law *even if you tell folktales.* Folktale plots cannot be copyrighted, but the particular words used to convey the plots can be copyrighted, and are the property of the copyright holder. There is no mechanical formula that can be applied to say when a different version is different enough. I have learned (the hard way) that I need to write into the contract that sources be given on tapes of my storytelling. Companies don't necessarily do that, even when the teller provides the information. The whole complex issue of copyright, permission, and giving credit to sources is a hot one in the storytelling community. It has been discussed in several articles and letters in *Storytelling Magazine* (and its predecessor, the *National Storytelling Journal*), the various storytelling newsletters, and in gatherings of tellers at the NAPPS Congresses and elsewhere. The discussion is by no means over. Read up and join in!

"Copyright and Storytelling," by Michael Skindrud. *National Storytelling Journal,* Winter 1984. An attorney discusses copyright issues. Available from NAPPS.

"Ethics in Storytelling." *National Storytelling Journal,* Fall 1987. A discussion from the Storytelling Congress that dealt with copyright, permission, giving credit. Available from NAPPS.

On Storytelling

Hamlet's speech to the players (Act III, Scene 2) is an excellent brief statement on technique that applies as well to storytelling as to acting.

Bauer, Caroline Feller. *Handbook for Storytellers.* American Library Association, 1977.
Media-oriented. Instructions on making flannelboards, telling stories on radio and TV, publicity for library programs. "Other Literary Sources" (pp.134-136) includes good ideas for finding stories to tell adults.

Breneman, Lucille N. and Bran Breneman. *Once Upon a Time: A Storytelling Handbook.* Nelson Hall, 1983.
This textbook for a storytelling class details general story preparation and contains a useful chapter on "Story Biography." "Short Stories for Storytelling" is an annotated bibliography of 31 stories (in short story collections for adults) that lend themselves to oral telling.

Colwell, Eileen. *A Storyteller's Choice.* Walck, 1964, o.p.
The stories are rather difficult, but the notes on how to tell (and sometimes cut) each story are illuminating. General discussion of storytelling pp. 203-208.

DeWit, Dorothy. *Children's Faces Looking Up.* American Library Association, 1979.
How to condense, expand, or retell a story; suggestions for theme programs.

Hamilton, Martha, Weiss, Mitch. *Children Tell Stories: A Teaching Guide.* Richard C. Owen, 1990. 135 Katonah Ave., Katonah, NY 10536.
Contains sensible tips for any teller.

Livo, Norma J. and Sandra A. Rietz. *Storytelling: Process and Practice.* Libraries Unlimited, 1986.
Don't feel you have to read all 450 pages before you can tell stories! However, this is a valuable book to refer to for specific needs: how and what to tell to different age groups, for instance (pp. 204-219). I also like their categories "Irritating Songs and Games" and "Infuriating Songs and Games."

MacDonald, Margaret Read. *Twenty Tellable Tales: Audience Participation Folk-tales for the Beginning Storyteller.* Wilson, 1986.
Includes sections on how to research and prepare stories and some hints on teaching storytelling to teachers, parents, and children.

Teresa Miller, compiler. *Joining In: An Anthology of Audience Participation Stories & How to Tell Them,* edited by Norma Livo. Yellow Moon, 1988.
A variety of stories contributed by various tellers, with participation instructions and comments by the tellers. The reader gets to watch storytellers think through their strategies and objectives for specific stories.

O'Callahan, Jay. *A Master Class in Storytelling.* Vineyard Video, Elias Lane, West Tisbury, MA 02575.
A 33-minute film/video that sets forth and illustrates the basics of storytelling in an entertaining and convincing way.

Pellowski, Anne. *The World of Storytelling: A Practical Guide to the Origins, Development and Applications of Storytelling.* Expanded and Revised Edition. Wilson, 1990.
Chronicles the variety of storytelling styles and functions worldwide.

Sawyer, Ruth. *The Way of the Storyteller.* Penguin, Revised edition, 1977, c.1942.
Mentor-in-a-book: excellent background on a storyteller's life, art, and sources. Watch out for the masculine representing both genders — there are "medicine-women" as well as "medicine-men" in traditional societies; there were female troubadors as well as male.

Smith, Jimmy Neil. *Homespun: Tales from America's Favorite Storytellers.* Crown, 1988.
Stories from the National Storytelling Festival with 42 pages on the craft of storytelling.

Stone, Kay F. "Oral Narration in Contemporary North America," in *Fairy Tales and Society: Illusion, Allusion and Paradigm* by Ruth B. Bottigheimer. University of Pennsylvania Press, 1986.
A folklorist compares three types of contemporary storytelling: traditional, non-traditional (librarian/teacher) and "neo-traditional" (professional).

Storytellers: Directory of Tellers, Festivals, Schools and Organizations

National Directory of Storytelling. NAPPS (National Association for the Preservation and Perpetuation of Storytelling), Box 309, Jonesborough, TN 37659. Where to find the Folktellers, Donald Davis, and about 400 other tellers. Includes all addresses and phone numbers, some tellers also list specialties. Also a long list of festivals, schools, organizations, and newsletters. NAPPS' own newsletter, the *Yarnspinner,* and their quarterly, *Storytelling Magazine,* list other festivals and workshops around the country and review resources. The magazine is included in their yearly membership of $25; the newsletter and the directory come with the $40 "membership plus."

Storytellers on Recordings, Film, Video

Storytelling Catalog from NAPPS, Box 309, Johesborough, TN 37659 lists selected tapes, records, films and videos of stories not read or recited by actors but told by storytellers. These items may be ordered from NAPPS. The catalog comes with a regular membership in NAPPS and a version is also send to many libraries. Included is *By Word of Mouth...Storytelling in America,* a 58-minute color video of the 1982 Tenth National Festival. Other sources are:
A Gentle Wind, Box 3103, Albany, NY 12203.
Appalshop, Box 743, Whitesburg, KY 41858.

Bibliography

Storytelling Center of Oneonta, P.O. Box 297, Oneonta, NY 13820, has available an extensive (though not annotated) bibliography of books and articles on many aspects of storytelling: technique, use in therapy and education, etc.

Periodicals

Association of Black Storytellers Newsletter.
ABS Editorial Board, P.O. Box 11484,
Baltimore, MD 21239.

*Fabula, Journal of Folktale
Studies.* 3/yr, 1958+. Berlin.

Jewish Storytelling Newsletter, c/o
Peninnah Schram, 525 West End Ave., 8C,
New York, NY 10024.

Journal of American Folklore.
q., 1888+. American Folklore Society.
Indexed in Humanities Index.

*Parabola — Myth and the Quest for
Meaning.* q., 1976+.

Sing Out! The Folk Song Magazine. q. Box
5253, Bethlehem, PA 18015. Regular
columns on storytelling ("The Endless
Tale" by Dan Keding) and on performing for/with children ("Kidsbeat" by
Sandy Byer).

Stories. q., 1987+. Katy Rydell, ed.
Newsletter of storytelling on the West
Coast. 12600 Woodbine St., Los Angeles,
CA 90066.

Storytelling Magazine, q., 1984+ (as
National Storytelling Journal), NAPPS,
Box 309, Jonesborough, TN 37659.

Other newsletters are listed
in the *National Directory of Storytelling.*

Teaching Storytelling

Hamilton, Martha, Weiss, Mitch.
Children Tell Stories: A Teaching Guide.
Richard C. Owen, 1990. [135 Katonah
Ave., Katonah, NY 10536.]
In consultation with many storytellers
and classroom teachers, the Beauty and
the Beast storytellers have written a truly
sensible guide to teaching storytelling
to children. Includes over 25 short, easy
stories.

On Folklore and Fairy Tales

Dégh, Linda. "The Nature of Feminine
Storytelling." *Folklore Women's Communi-
cations* (newsletter of the Women's Section of the American Folklore Society),
38-39 (1986): 4-9.
Among European peasant tellers studied,
women, like men, tend to tell more hero
tales than heroine tales, but women
emphasize feelings and description of
women's everyday lives.

Kolbenschlag, Madonna. *Kiss Sleeping
Beauty Goodbye.* Harper, 1988 (c. 1981).
Analysis of a group of popular tales that
exhibit a range of negative to positive
images of women.

Rooth, Anna Birgitta. *The Importance of
Storytelling: A Study Based on Field Work
in Northern Alaska.* Studia Ethnologica
Upsaliensia, 1976.

Interesting anecdotes in this pamphlet
reveal the function of storytelling in the
daily lives and religion of Inuits and Indians, and their expectations of the storyteller.

Seitel, Peter. *See So That We May See: Per-
formances and Interpretations of Traditional
Tales from Tanzania.* Indiana U. Press,
1980.

Sexton, Anne. *Transformations.*
Houghton, 1971.
Psychological implications of Grimm
tales explored in poetry. Briefer and more
convincing (to me) than Bettelheim's *The
Uses of Enchantment.*

Stone, Elizabeth. *Black Sheep & Kissing
Cousins: How Our Family Stories Shape
Us.* Times Books, 1988.

Tolkien, J.R.R. *Tree and Leaf.* Houghton,
1965.
"On Fairy Tales" (pp. 3-84) is an essay on
the "sub-creation" of fantasy worlds with
their own rules, whose workings reflect
values in our own world.

Wolkstein, Diane. *The Magic Orange Tree
and Other Haitian Folktales.* Knopf, 1978.
Each story is introduced by a description
of the circumstances under which Wolkstein collected it—who was telling, to
whom, how, and what the audience reaction was.

Zeitlin, Steven J., Amy J. Kotkin and
Holly Cutting Baker. *A Celebration of
American Family Folklore: Tales and
Traditions from the Smithsonian Collection.*
Pantheon, 1982.
Fascinating family anecdotes and how
they function in family dynamics.

CHOOSING THE MEDIUM

SO FAR, I HAVE TALKED about using spoken words, gestures and silence to tell stories. They are sufficient. However, singing, chanting, dancing, pictures, puppets, paperfolding, or a bit of play-acting can be added to put variety into a storytelling session or to attract attention in a distracting situation. Each of these embellishments is traditional in some culture, somewhere. They are only untraditional if you use them in a story from a culture where they are not traditional. But then, there are cultures where telling a story while standing stock still would be distinctly untraditional.

Many tellers begin by reading stories aloud, with or without showing the pictures. All that applies to telling applies here—phrasing, pace, even some eye contact—so ideally the story should be rehearsed, even though it is not learned or memorized. A pitfall in reading aloud is launching into a sentence and then realizing you have put the emphasis on the wrong word. Only a rehearsal—even a silent one—can prevent this.

People disagree about showing pictures with a story. Some prefer to leave the illustration of the story to the listeners' imagination (which they feel is all too rarely exercised). Some stories are so rich in language, imagery, ideas, that adding a visual element would only take away from the aural experience. Bettelheim adds that a monster imagined by the listener may have useful psychological meaning, while the illustrator's monster "may scare us without evoking any deeper meaning beyond anxiety."* Others feel that the picture book program is an opportunity to introduce young children to excellent art, and want to show the pictures along with the story, or at least right afterwards.

Some picture books, like *Rosie's Walk*, have half the story in the pictures and can't be used without them. Some, like *Mommy, Buy Me a China Doll*, are long and repetitious, which is fine for bedtime but may fall flat in storytime without the added interest of the pictures. Some, like *Whose Mouse Are You?* have pictures that are just too much fun to do without (the illustrations in this one appeal as much to a high school child development class as to a preschool group). There are other books I would use without the pictures because they are too small or delicate to be seen at a distance, or because I feel the pictures are sexist or racist, defects more common to illustrations than to the texts they illustrate.

When you begin, it is good to practice reading and showing picture books in front of a friend or a mirror to see if the pictures really can be seen. Common faults are holding the book at a slant so the pictures are aimed mainly at the ceiling, covering some crucial part of the picture with a finger, and going too fast, especially if the text is brief. I find the first page of the story so I am not awkwardly leafing through dedications and copyright notices, then hold the book up to the side with the top about level with my shoulder. Warning: check for pitfalls like a picture oriented end-ways in an otherwise side-ways book, or a picture that gives away the punch line before you get to it in the text—this last may require memorizing a line or two to permit you to turn the page at the proper moment.

Holding up a book the proper way can give you incentive to do a "stretch" in the middle of a program, but you can have your stretch and the story too if you don't use the book at all. *Caps for Sale* without the book becomes an audience participa-

---

The Uses of Enchantment: The Meaning and Importance of Fairy Tales by Bruno Bettelheim (Knopf, 1976), pp. 59-60.

tion story. I shake my fist at the monkeys, and the audience, with only the slightest encouragement, shakes its fists at the peddler.

Then there are a few stories, like *The Three Billy Goats Gruff,* that go over well in any medium, and are in such demand that a variety of media does more to prevent boredom in the teller than in the listener. There's a book with large, bold, appealing, not-too-scary illustrations by Marcia Brown, and the story lends itself to puppets, pantomime, and creative dramatics. It is perfect for finger puppets. The left hand is the bridge and the left arm the hillside (if you are right-handed). The troll puppet, on the left thumb, hides under the bridge and pops up at the "up" of "gobble you up!" The goats are played by the first, middle and little fingers of the right hand (ring fingers are not nimble enough to play goats).

The Fat Cat has illustrations I love, but I have been won away by another method of telling. I narrate the story and play the woodcutter. My accomplice, with a sheet tied around her neck, plays the cat and chooses the rest of the cast from the audience, while I coach them. In a few minutes we are ready to start. As I narrate the story, the players one by one recite their one line, "What have you been eating, my little cat? You are so fat!" One by one the cat tells them what she has already eaten and then "eats" them by throwing the sheet over them. Older children always cooperate spontaneously, though we don't tell them what is going to happen. Younger ones should be at the end of the line so they are not surprised. They may need some coaxing from the friendly cat. If they don't go in, or if they come out again to see what the growing cat looks like, that is part of the fun.

Margot Zemach's *It Could Always Be Worse* (Farrar Straus, 1977) can be dramatized even more simply than *The Fat Cat,* and there's no danger of frightening even the youngest participants. Either I tell the story alone, or I am the narrator and the man whose house was too small and an accomplice, with very little preparation, is the rabbi. I bring the children on stage, as the story progresses, to be the family and the animals, doing sound effects, of course. I say "He ran out of the house and slammed the door" and clap or stamp to cue the children to stop

the sound effects while I talk to the rabbi. I would do only one of these on-stage participation stories in a program, and put it near the end, as they are pretty heady stuff. They are especially good for family programs.

A more refined kind of dramatized storytelling is tandem telling. The first tandem storytelling I heard was at the Jonesborough festival, in 1975, from the Roadside Theater and from the Folktellers. It is a form halfway between telling and dramatization. Two (or more) tellers alternate narrating a story, and take different characters' parts during dialogue. It is not a play, because there is still much narration, and there need be no props, no costumes and very little movement beyond the gestures tellers would use anyway. It is more theatrical than solo telling, however, and is well suited to provide variety and excitement in a stage program such as a school assembly. By eliminating a lot of "he said" and "she said" it can step up the pace of a story. At its best it sounds like two friends so eager to tell you something that they are interrupting each other. In fact, it is best done by friends whose style is similar enough to blend into one narration.

The stories that best translate into tandem telling either have two main characters ("Ticoumba and the President," Arnold Lobel's Frog and Toad stories, Harve Zemach's *Penny a Look*), or one main character who interacts with a series of minor characters one at a time, as in "The Gingerbread Boy" or Zemach's *The Judge: An Untrue Tale.* The former also work well as two-hand-puppet stories, and the latter work well as flannelboard stories.

Flannelboard takes time to prepare well, so the stories should be chosen with care. Cloth or felt cut-out figures will stick to a board covered with flannel, so figures can be redrawn from a book too small to use with a group, and displayed on the board as they come into the narrative. This works best with cumulative stories or songs, where the figures can be added and/or taken off in succession, or for stories with a very simple cast and plot. Otherwise the teller has to pay more attention to the board than to the telling or the audience. Cumulative stories lend themselves well to audience participation: dole out the figures and have the audience put them on the board. I don't use flannelboards, so if you want to know more, see Judy Sierra's *Flannel Board Storytelling Book* or Caroline Bauer's *Handbook for Storytellers*.

Some good stories using props are "The Yam Thief," a string trick story useful for catching the attention of older children dubious about listening to stories, and the drawing story in *On the Banks of Plum Creek* by Laura Ingalls Wilder (p. 318). The same string trick used in "The Yam Thief" can illustrate *The Mitten*, a Ukrainian story for younger children. Two paper folding stories follow on pages 22 and 26.

To me, the most fascinating and beautiful visual storytelling is storytelling in American Sign Language. If you can find someone who signs and has time to practice with you, you can do a program of interest to both hearing and deaf audiences. Practicing beforehand is necessary for three reasons: the signer can do a more creative interpretation if he or she is familiar with the story, you can adjust your pace to the needs of the signer, and you won't be so distracted by the signing if your curiosity is satisfied during rehearsal.

Another way of presenting stories is by singing them. Ballads can be used on their own or as introductions to books in which they are illustrated or retold in prose (Joseph Jacobs has retold several). *Folksong in the Classroom* (c/o John W. Scott, P.O. Box 264, Holyoke, MA 10141), a newsletter with songs on a different topic in each issue, can help you find songs to go in theme programs. Their article "Troubled Children and Bad People Ballads" (Spring 1990) is especially helpful. Children's Music Network (P.O. Box 307, Montvale, New Jersey 07645) is an organization that includes storytellers as well as musicians, teachers, parents and children. Its newsletter, *Pass It On*, has new songs, articles on performing and songwriting for/with children, notices of new recordings, and a page by children.

Some stories come with songs already in them. Folklorists call them *cante fable*, and they are traditional in many countries. "Barney McCabe," "The Foolish Frog," "Fiddler, Play Fast, Play Faster," "Owl" and "Nine-in-One, Grr! Grr!" are listed in Sisters' Choices; books with several *cante fable* in them are listed at the end of this chapter.

You don't need a great voice or perfect pitch to sing in story programs. A simple instrument such as an autoharp can help you stay on key, or you can sing along with a record or tape. (Just playing a recording without singing along won't encourage audience participation, though it's all right for background music before the program starts.) Young children are a good audience to start on. They aren't too critical about tone or pitch; they respond mainly to rhythm. If you aren't holding an instrument, you can choose a picture-book song and show the pictures as you sing. A song or chant with hand motions can be a welcome break in a children's story hour, when the little ones get wiggly and your arms are cramped from holding up a picture book. For older children and adults, music also provides a break in the sense that it requires a different kind of focus from storytelling.

These are some of the different ways in which a story can be told. No storyteller needs to know all of them. Many tellers and listeners prefer straight oral telling and they need nothing more. I like to have a choice of media ready for special occasions.

Which medium to use depends on the audience as well as the story. Straight telling can be used with any size group, as can drawing stories. A small audience also enjoys finger puppets, string stories, paperfolding and picture books. A large audience will respond to the largest picture books, flannelboards, paperfolding and to hand puppets used without a stage. For a very large audience, *large* puppets work, and dramatized storytelling such as *The Fat Cat* or shadowplays. I don't usually do a whole program with props and special effects unless the audience is large, unruly, and unused to storytelling. Generally, even in a distracting situation like an outdoor fair I can do a few visual stories to attract an audience and focus attention, and then do some plain oral telling as well.

Whether you ever use props with storytelling depends also on what feels comfortable to you. Some beginners find that a guitar or a string trick gives them something to do with their hands and makes them feel easier about facing an audience. Others find props just something extra to think about when they would rather concentrate on the telling.

✠✠

Simple Picture Books

Barton, Byron. *Bones, Bones, Dinosaur Bones.* Crowell, 1990.

Brown, Margaret Wise. *Goodnight Moon,* illus. Clement Hurd. Harper, 1947.

Burningham, John. *Mr. Gumpy's Outing.* Holt, 1971.

Dodds, Dayle Ann. *Wheel Away!* illus. Thacher Hurd. Harper, 1989.

Greenfield, Eloise. *Africa Dream,* illus. Carole Byard. Day, 1977.
This is simple to present but works for older children.

Hutchins, Pat. *Rosie's Walk.* Macmillan, 1968.

Kraus, Robert. *Whose Mouse Are You?* illus. Jose Aruego. Macmillan, 1970.

Sendak, Maurice. *The Nutshell Library: Chicken Soup with Rice, One Was Johnny, Pierre,* Harper, 1962.

Walsh, Ellen S. *Mouse Paint.* Harcourt, 1989.

Weiss, Nicki. *Where Does the Brown Bear Go?* Greenwillow, 1989.

Williams, Garth. *The Chicken Book: A Traditional Rhyme.* Doubleday, 1990.

Williams, Vera B. *More More More Said the Baby.* Greenwillow, 1990.

Longer Picture Books

Asbjornsen, Peter C. *The Three Billy Goats Gruff,* illus. Marcia Brown. Harcourt, 1957, pbk. 1972.

Babbitt, Natalie. *Nellie: A Cat on Her Own.* Farrar, 1989.

Bemelmens, Ludwig. *Madeline.* Viking, 1939.

Carlstrom, Nancy White. *Wild Wild Sunflower Child Anna,* illus. Jerry Pinkney. Macmillan, 1987.

Cooney, Barbara. *Miss Rumphius.* Puffin, 1982.

Fox, Mem. *Wilfrid Gordon McDonald Partridge,* illus. Julie Vivas. Kane/Miller, 1985.

Hall, Donald. *Ox-cart Man,* illus. Barbara Cooney. Viking Penguin, 1979.

Herman, Emily. *Hubknuckles.* Crown, 1985. Halloween.

Keats, Ezra Jack. *Peter's Chair.* Harper, 1967.

Krauss, Ruth. *A Very Special House,* illus. Maurice Sendak. Harper, 1953.

Le Guin, Ursula K. *A Visit from Dr. Katz,* illus. Ann Barrow. Atheneum, 1988.

Lionni, Leo. *Tillie and the Wall.* Knopf, 1990.

Luenn, Nancy. *Nessa's Fish,* illus. Neil Waldman. Atheneum, 1990.

Marshall, James. *The Cut-Ups.* Viking Kestrel, 1984.

McKissack, Patricia. *Flossie and the Fox,* illus. Rachel Isadora. Dial, 1986.

Polacco, Patricia. *Thunder Cake.* Philomel, 1990.

Ringgold, Faith. *Tar Beach.* Crown, 1991.

Sendak, Maurice. *Where the Wild Things Are.* Harper, 1963.

Yolen, Jane. *Owl Moon,* illus. John Schoenherr. Philomel, 1987.

Participation Picture Books

Aardema, Verna. *Why Mosquitoes Buzz in People's Ears: A West African Tale,* illus. Diane and Leo Dillon. Dial, 1975.

Elting, Mary and Michael Folsom. *Q is for Duck, An Alphabet Guessing Game,* illus. Jack Kent. Houghton, 1980.

Gág, Wanda. *Millions of Cats.* Coward, 1928.

Hill, Eric. *Where's Spot?* Putnam, 1980. (A Lift-the-Flap Book).

Hoban, Tana. *Look Again.* Macmillan, 1971.

Kent, Jack. *The Fat Cat, a Danish Folktale.* Scholastic, 1972.

Martin, Bill and John Archambault. *Chicka Chicka Boom Boom,* illus. Lois Ehlert. Simon & Schuster, 1989.

Marzollo, Jean. *Pretend You're a Cat,* illus. Jerry Pinkney. Dial, 1990.

Miller, Margaret. *Who Uses This?* Greenwillow, 1990.

Robart, Rose. *The Cake That Mack Ate,* illus. Maryann Kovalski. Joy Street/Little, Brown, 1986.

Shaw, Charles. *It Looked Like Spilt Milk.* Harper, 1947.

Zemach, Harve. *The Judge: An Untrue Tale,* illus. Margot Zemach. Farrar, 1969.

Zemach, Harve. *Mommy, Buy Me a China Doll,* illus. Margot Zemach. Farrar, 1966.

Picture Books to Sing

Animal Song, illus. Marcia Sewall. Little Brown, 1988.

The Cat Goes Fiddle-I-Fee, illus. Paul Galdone. Clarion, 1985.
Music not included, but can be found in Jane Yolen's *Fireside Song Book of Birds and Beasts.*

The Fox Went Out on a Chilly Night, illus. Peter Spier. Doubleday, 1961.
I paperclip the pages together so I only show the color spreads, not the too-small black-and-white pictures between. That makes the page-turning rhythm match the music.

Hurd, Thacher. *Mama Don't Allow.* Harper, 1984.
Music included for "Mama Don't Allow" but you may want to make up a simple tune for the lullaby. Cante fable.

Hush Little Baby, illus. Aliki. Prentice-Hall, 1968.

Reynolds, Malvina. *Morningtown Ride.* Turn-the-Page Press, 1984.

Shannon, George. *Lizard's Song,* illus. Jose Aruego and Ariane Dewey. Greenwillow, 1981.

Skip to My Lou, illus. Nadine Bernard Westcott. Joy Street, 1989.
Repeat lines to make each page a verse so the illustrations don't whip by too fast.

Staines, Bill. *All God's Critters Got a Place in the Choir,* illus. Margot Zemach. Dutton, 1989.

Xiong, Blia. *Nine-in-One Grr! Grr! A Folktale from the Hmong People of Laos,* illus. Nancy Hom. Children's Book Press, 1989.
Make up the simplest tune for Tiger's song.

Cante Fable

East, Helen. *The Singing Sack*. London: A & C Black, 1989. [Available from World Music Press, P.O. Box 2565, Danbury, CT 06813.]
28 song stories from 19 countries, with accompanying tape. Stories in English, songs in original language.

Serwadda, W. Moses. *Songs and Stories from Uganda*. Thomas Y. Crowell, 1974. [Available from World Music.]

Wolkstein, Diane. *The Magic Orange Tree and Other Haitian Folktales*. Knopf, 1978. Many of the stories include chants or songs.

Song Recordings

All for Freedom. Sweet Honey in the Rock. Music for Little People.
Spirited songs celebrating freedom, ethnic diversity and being alive.

American Folk Songs for Children. Pete Seeger. Folkways FTS 31501.
From Ruth Crawford Seeger's book. All his other children's recordings too.

Lirica Infantil, v. 1-3. Jose-Luis Orozco. Arco Iris Records, P.O.Box 7428, Berkeley, CA 94707.
Easy-to-lead songs, chants and singing games from Latin America. Lyrics and translations included.

Our Record. Tom Hunter. Long Sleeve, 22 Eugene, Mill Valley, CA 94941.
Tom's songs give a child's-eye view of light and heavy subjects.

Pizza Boogie. Joanne Olshansky and The Brontosaurus Chorus Kids. JHO Music, 11 Marshall Terrace, Wayland, MA 01778.
Good ideas in high energy songs.

Plum Pudding: Stories and Songs with Nancy Schimmel and the Plum City Players. Audio cassette or LP. Sisters' Choice, 1982.
Also their *Dinosaur and Other Songs from Plum City*.

Rabbits Dance: Marcia Berman Sings Malvina Reynolds. B/B Records, 570 N Arden Blvd., Los Angeles, CA 90004.
Excellent musicians and arrangements, songs for pre-school and primary grades.

Really Rosie. Ode.
Composed and sung by Carole King, words from Maurice Sendak's Nutshell Library.

Songwriting Together: Cooperative Songwriting to Build Closeness with the Earth and Each Other. Audio cassette. Sarah Pirtle, 54 Thayer Road, Greenfield, MA 01301.
A tape of 22 songs with 17 song patterns for children to create their own songs. Includes a teacher's guide, lyrics, guitar chords, and complete lesson plans for songwriting in small cooperative groups using a whole-language approach.

Step It Down. Bessie Jones. LP or cassette. Rounder. Available from World Music Press, P. O. Box 2565, Danbury, CT 06813.
18 selections from Bessie Jones' book and 26 page booklet by Mary Jo Sanna.

Sharing Thoughts. Compiled by Andrea Stone. Audio cassette. Stone Productions, Box 307, Montvale, NJ 07645-0307.
A collection of songs for kids by various contemporary singer/songwriters about issues related to getting along with others. A Group Leader's/Educator's Guide Book which offers ideas, guidelines for facilitating discussions, and activities to go with each song is also available.

Through Children's Eyes. The Limelighters. RCA.
Includes my favorite participation song, "Join into the Game."

Uncle Ruthie. Ruth Buell, 1731 S. Sherbourne Drive, Los Angeles, CA 90035.
Her country-western babysitting song, "Why Did You Leave Me?" should become a classic.

We All Have a Song: Activity and Bed-time Songs with Ginni Clemmens. Folkways.
An audience-participation record. Try it.

Whoever Shall Have Some Good Peanuts. Sam Hinton. Folkways.
Title cut is a good song for a group to rewrite.

World Music Press P.O. Box 2565, Danbury, CT 06813 is a good source for recordings and books of songs and singing games from many countries.

A Gentle Wind, Box 3103, Albany, NY 12203, has a line of children's music and storytelling tapes, including good stuff by Guy Carawan, Betsy Rose, Ruth Pelham.

Songbooks

Reynolds, Malvina. *Tweedles and Foodles for Young Noodles*. Schroder, 1961. Pre-school/primary songs.

Seeger, Ruth Crawford. *American Folk Songs for Children*. Doubleday, c. 1948. Folk songs for pre-school and primary grades and how to use them, presented by a composer, teacher and folklorist.

Winn, Marie. *The Fireside Book of Children's Songs*. Simon & Schuster, 1966. The good old camp songs and other songs for grade 3 and up.

Winn, Marie. *The Fireside Book of Fun and Game Songs*. Simon & Schuster, 1974. Familiar songs for pre-school on up.

Visual Stories

Pellowski, Anne. *The Story Vine: A Source Book of Unusual and Easy-to-Tell Stories from Around the World*. Macmillan, 1984. String, drawing and finger-play stories, and two stories using thumb piano. Her *Family Storytelling Handbook* has additional visual stories.

Sierra, Judy. *The Flannel Board Storytelling Book*. Wilson, 1987. Simple tales, songs and poems with instructions and patterns for flannelboard use.

Tompert, Ann. *Grandfather Tang's Story*, illus. Robert Andrew Parker. Crown, 1990.
A transformation-chase story illustrated with tangrams.

Fingerpuppets

Dorothy Tharpe, 73 East Teresa Street, Roberts, WI 54023, (715) 749-4094. Send for price list for puppets and patterns. These knit puppets of story characters are easy to use because they cling to the fingers.

AN ASSORTMENT OF STORIES

"THE PANCAKE" IS AN OLD Norwegian nursery tale that appears in several collections. Gay Ducey and I have re-worked it for tandem telling (as described in "Choosing the Medium" page 16). Dialogue is in roman type, narration in italic. Pace is particularly important in this story. We start easy, then speed up a lot and overlap in the chase scene, ease off for the transition, overlap some in the dialogue, slow for the exchange with the pig, and eat the pancake as quickly as possible.

"The Rainhat" is a traditional paper folding story; I have seen three versions. I learned mine from a girl, about nine, who was telling it to a librarian when I dropped into a library in San Francisco around 1970. I changed the boy in her story to a girl, as I wasn't finding enough girls in children's adventure stories, but I told the story for many months before I realized I was saying "fireman's helmet" instead of "firefighter's helmet." The same folds, without the story, can be found in H. A. Rey's *Curious George Rides a Bike* (Houghton, 1952). A small group of first graders or a class of second graders can learn these folds, or most of them.

Another visual story, "The Handsome Prince," I made up to go with traditional Chinese folds taught to me by Elizabeth Sor when I worked with her at the San Mateo County Library. The instructions following the story show the figures in succession as they appear in the story. This story is difficult for one person to fold and tell at the same time; Elizabeth and I did it together for fifteen branch libraries before I was able to do it alone. For this reason, I put the story on my videotape (see Sisters' Choices). I use the story to introduce the art of Chinese and Japanese (origami) paperfolding to children from the third grade up. For the third grade, I don't teach all the figures.

If you want to go on with paperfolding, some easy-to-teach figures are found in these books:

Folding Paper Toys by Shari Lewis and Lillian Oppenheimer. Scarborough House, 1963. See bugcatcher (fortune-teller), house and couch and bureau. The jumping frog is not easy, but recycles old catalog cards (while the supply lasts).

Origami Toys by Toshie Takahama. C. B Tuttle, 1973. See ko-tong-kong, "The Captain's Shirt" (a version of "The Rainhat"), leaping frog (slightly simpler than Lewis'). Also includes finger puppets.

Traditional origami paper is cut exactly square, white on one side and colored on the other. The color is helpful for teaching and satisfying to use. Origami paper is available from The Origami Center of America, 31 Union Square, New York, NY 10003. The center also carries origami books. Send a large stamped, self-addressed envelope for their price list. Earth Care Paper (P.O. Box 7070, Madison, WI 53707) now lists origami paper made out of recycled paper. I haven't tried it yet.

I made up "A Story for Heather" as I drove down the Blue Ridge Parkway after a visit with Guy, Candie and Heather Carawan, the musical family who first took me to the National Storytelling Festival in Jonesborough. I passed a turnoff to the town of Crossnore and began to wonder what a crossnore was. The story is the answer. It contains no songs or visual elements. Crossnores don't like them.

"The Lionmakers" is my retelling of a tale from the Panchatantra, a collection used for the education of princes in India, circa 500 CE, and available in a translation by Arthur Ryder (University of Chicago

Press, 1964). Different versions have been published in Harold Courlander's *The Tiger's Whisker* and in Rose Dobbs' *Once Upon a Time,* but both books are out of print. I tell it on *Tell Me a Story: Nancy Schimmel* from Kartes Videocommunications.

The story goes equally well in an environmental or a peace program, and appears on both lists. It also proved useful when I was telling to a group of sixth grade classes on the penultimate day of school while their teachers took turns going elsewhere to fill out their report cards.

A STORY FOR HEATHER

ONCE THERE WAS A LITTLE girl named Heather. Every morning she drove the goats to pasture, through the valley and up the hillside to the meadow, and every evening she drove them home again. As she walked along behind the goats, she always sang, songs she learned from her mother and father and songs she made up herself. In the morning she sang because she was happy and rested and ready for anything. In the evening she sang because a song is good company when you're alone with the goats and the shadows.

What Heather didn't know was that every day, as she walked through the valley, she walked right over a crossnore that lived under the ground—or rather I should say lived in the ground, for a crossnore moves through the ground like a shark through the sea or a tiger through the jungle. What they look like, nobody knows, for they never come out of the ground. This crossnore never moved far, though he wondered if the next valley might be better than his. He was always wanting to find out, but always wanting to get a good long sleep before he started, so he would be rested and ready for anything. And some meadowlark or thrush by day, some nightingale or melodious frog by night, was always waking him up in the middle of his good long sleep. Crossnores hate music. It always wakes

them up, and the prettier the song, the more it wakes them up.

And the most annoying times in this crossnore's whole day were when he heard the trip-trap of the goats' hoofs (which he didn't mind at all) and then Heather's high, clear voice singing some beautiful song (which he minded awfully). He longed to grab Heather by her little bare toes and drag her into the ground and stop up her mouth with dirt, but her voice was so clear and sweet that he couldn't bear to get close enough to do it. So he bided his time, and grumbled.

Then, one day, the goats passed overhead, and the pad-pad-pad of little bare feet, but the crossnore did not hear any singing. Heather had a cold and could not sing a note. In the morning, the crossnore was too surprised to catch her, but all day long, as he muttered at thrushes and shouldered sharp stones out of his bed, he plotted and planned to grab Heather's little bare toes and drag her under the ground that very night.

And all day long, Heather thought how lonely it would be, walking home through the evening shadows without a song for company. In the evening, when she started down the path, she still couldn't sing. At the head of the valley, she passed a clump of willows. She took out her knife and snicked off a piece of willow as she went by, and started to whittle as she walked. And as she walked, the crossnore waited, and listened, and soon he heard the trip-trap of the goats' hoofs, and the pad-pad-pad of Heather's little bare feet, but just as he grabbed for her little bare toes, she raised her new-made willow whistle to her lips and blew the clearest, sweetest tune the crossnore had ever heard. He dove straight down into the earth so fast the ground sank three feet right under Heather, and Heather sank with it. She climbed out of the hole and whistled her way home, and the crossnore moved to the next valley and never came back.

When Heather got home, she told her mother and father what had happened to her. They told her a nice story about underground streams and sinkholes, and she almost believed it, but she won't really know what happened until she hears the story of How Heather Whistled Away the Crossnore.

THE RAINHAT

ONE DAY A LITTLE GIRL wanted to go out to play, but her mother wouldn't let her because it was raining so hard. The little girl didn't want to stay in the house because all she had to play with was an old piece of paper. She didn't have crayons or scissors so she took the paper and she folded it and folded it, waiting for the rain to stop, but it didn't, so she folded it some more and she made herself a rainhat and put it on and went outside anyway.

The first thing she saw was a house burning down. That fire was so hot it was burning even in the rain. And she wanted to help put out the fire, but she didn't think she could do that...wearing a rainhat. So she took off the rainhat and folded it and folded it and made a firefighter's helmet. She put it on and she was ready to take care of the fire. She poured on water and poured on water until the fire was all out. She poured on so much water that she made a flood. And then she wanted to go sailing on the flood. But she wouldn't go sailing in a firefighter's hat, so she took it off and folded it and folded it and made a pirate hat. She put on the pirate hat and she was ready to go sailing ...except...she needed a boat.

So she took off the pirate hat and folded it and folded it and made a boat. She got in the boat and started to sail over the flood. But you know, floods are dangerous. The water is all muddy and the little girl couldn't see what was under it. So she ran into a house, and broke the bow off the boat. But that didn't stop her. She just turned the boat around and kept sailing. Then she ran into a store, and broke the stern off the boat. But the little girl was brave, and she kept sailing. Then she crashed into the library (or the building you are in, if you're in one) and broke a hole right in the middle of the boat. Well, with a hole right in the middle of the boat, what happened to the boat?* That's right, it sank. But the little girl didn't drown, because she was wearing a lifejacket.

*Here is an exception to an otherwise reliable rule: Never ask a question during a story unless you are willing to take an irrelevant reply and run with it, because that's what you'll get. But this question is well enough set up (don't just say 'what happened?' say 'what happened to the boat?') so that so far it has always elicited the right answer.

1.
Fold rectangular paper in half

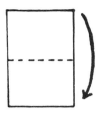

2.
Fold again and unfold to make crease

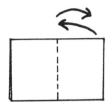

3.
Bring top fold down along crease

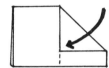

4.
Fold other side to match

5.
Fold one flap up

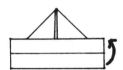

6.
Turn over and fold other flap

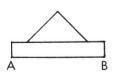

7.
Open rainhat, pulling till A touches B

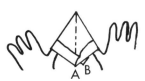

8.
Tuck one bottom flap
behind the other

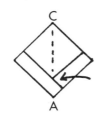

9.
Fold front up so
A touches C

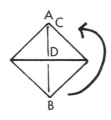

10.
Open up to firefighter's helmet

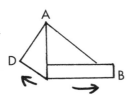

11.
Close again

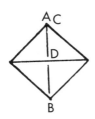

12.
Turn over,
fold B up to C

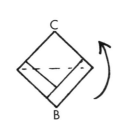

13.
Pirate hat

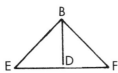

14.
Open pirate hat,
pull till E touches F

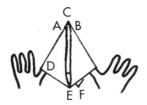

15.
Pinch A and B

16.
Pull A and B out

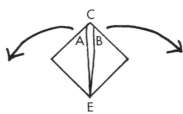

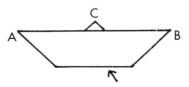

17.
Crease bottom
fold of boat

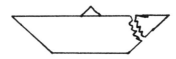

18.
Tear off bow

19.
Turn boat around,
tear off stern

20.
Tear off peak,
show hole, lower boat

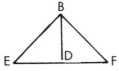

21.
Unfold to life jacket
(shoulders still folded),
raise jacket

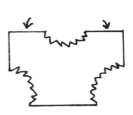

THE PANCAKE

C: *One morning, a goodwife was cooking a sweet milk pancake over the fire. The pancake lay in the pan, frizzling away, so beautiful and thick, it was a pleasure to look at. The children were standing 'round the fire, and the goodman sat in the corner and looked on. The pancake smelled so good that the children started begging for a bite.*

P: Please, mother, give me a bite of pancake, *said one.*

C: Please, dear mother, give me a bite of pancake, *said the second.*

P: Please, dear, good mother, give me a bite of pancake, *said the third.*

C: Please, dear, good, kind mother, give me a bite of pancake, *said the fourth.*

P: Please, dear, good, kind, sweet mother, give me a bite of pancake, *said the fifth.*

C: Please, dear, good, kind, sweet, generous mother, give me a bite of pancake, *said the sixth.*

P: Please, dear, good, kind, sweet, generous, clever mother, give me a bite of pancake, *said the seventh.*

C: *And each one begged more prettily than the other, for they were so very hungry,*

P: *and they were such good children.*

C: Yes, dears, but it is not done yet. You must wait until it turns itself.

P: *Now, she should not have said 'wait until it turns itself,'*

C: *she should have said 'wait until I turn the pancake,' for the pancake lay in the pan and thought,*

P: must I turn myself?

C: *And the pancake tried to turn itself*

P: *but it was too soft.*

C: *So it waited until it had cooled a bit longer, and was firmer in the flesh, and then it tried again*

P: *and it turned itself right over.*

C: *And when it had cooked a little while on the other side, and was all golden brown, it was so strong*

P: *that it jumped right out of the pan and started rolling across the floor like a wheel.*

C: Stop, Pancake! *cried the goodwife, running after it.*

P: *But the Pancake rolled right out the door.*

C: Stop, pancake! *cried the goodman, running after the goodwife,*

P: *but the Pancake rolled down the path and out the gate.*

C: Stop, Pancake! *cried the seven hungry children, running after the goodman,*

P: *but the Pancake rolled down the road and soon left them far behind.*

C: *After a while,*

P: *the Pancake met a hen.*

C: Good morning, Pancake, *said the hen.*

P: Good morning, Henny Penny, *said the pancake, and kept rolling.*

C: Pancake, dear, don't roll so fast! Bide a bit and let me eat you.

P: Oh, no! I ran away from the goodwife and her goodman and their seven squalling children and I shall run away from you too, Henny Penny.

C: *The Pancake rolled on*

P: *until it met a duck.*

C: Good morning, Pancake.

P: Good morning, Ducky Lucky, *said the pancake, and kept rolling.*

C: Pancake, dear, don't roll so fast. Bide a bit and let me eat you.

P: Oh, no! I ran away from the goodwife and her goodman and their seven squalling children and Henny Penny, and I shall run away from you too, Ducky Lucky.

C: *The pancake rolled on*

P: *until it met a goose.*

C: Good morning, Pancake.

P: Good morning, Goosey Loosey, *said the pancake, and kept rolling.*

C: Pancake, dear, don't roll so fast. Bide a bit and let me eat you.

P: Oh, no! I ran away from the goodwife and her goodman and their seven squalling children and Henny Penny and Ducky Lucky, and I shall run away from you too, Goosey Loosey.

C: *And the pancake rolled on*

P: *until it came to a pig.*

C: Good morning, pancake.

P: Good morning, Piggy Wiggy, *said the pancake, and rolled faster than ever.*

C: Nay, wait a bit, you needn't be in such a hurry. I see you are coming to the woods, and they say it isn't very safe there. We two should travel together and keep each other company.

P: Well, there may be something in that. *So the pancake slowed down.*

C: *and the pig trotted up,*

P & C: *and side by side they entered the woods, and side by side they went along*

P: *until they came to a stream.*

C: *The pig was nice and fat and could swim very well, but the pancake said,*

P: How can I get across? I cannot swim at all.

C: Hop on my snout, and I'll carry you across.

P: *The pancake did so.*

C: *And the pig carried it to the middle of the stream, and then, Ouf! Ouf! he tossed the pancake in the air, caught it in his mouth, and swallowed it in a gulp.*

P: *And as the pancake cannot go any farther,*

C: *The story can't go any farther either.*

THE LIONMAKERS

FOUR MEN GREW UP TOGETHER in a little village in India. Three of the men were scholars, but the fourth man never studied anything. In fact, he had never read a book in his life. He just got along as best he could on his own common sense. But the four men had been friends as children, and they remained friends despite their differences.

One day, the four friends were sitting under the trees talking of this and that when one of the scholars said, "Something has been bothering me. I have spent all my life studying, and I know many things, but I know them only from books. I don't know if my knowledge works, out in the world."

"You know," said another of the scholars, "the same thing has been bothering me! But somehow, this little village doesn't seem to offer the scope for me to try out my vast knowledge."

"Clearly," said the third scholar, "we must travel out into the world and try out our knowledge there." The other scholars agreed, but then there was their friend. They had always done everything together, share and share alike, but suppose…suppose they found some lost treasure by using their knowledge? Suppose they solved a problem for a rajah and he rewarded them with gold and jewels? They had studied late into the night to prepare themselves for this work, and their friend had done nothing. He had only common sense, and what rajah would be impressed with that? They argued this back and forth, as they so enjoyed doing, but finally they decided to do as they had always done, share and share alike.

And so they started on their journey. They walked along for many days, and one day they saw some bones scattered by the path. One of the scholars said, "I can tell from my studies that these bones are the bones of a lion. Now it happens that I have learned how to arrange the bones as they would be in a living lion."

"Really?" said the second scholar, "that is interesting — for it happens that from my studies I know how to clothe the bones with flesh and blood and skin and fur."

"Indeed?" said the third scholar. "How curious. It happens that I know the next step. Once the animal is formed, I know how to breathe the breath of life into it. Clearly, this is the place where we should try out our knowledge to see if it works in the world." The others agreed.

The fourth man, the one who wasn't a scholar, was simply struck dumb by this display of learning and didn't say anything at all.

So the first scholar stepped forward and arranged the bones as they would be in a living lion. Then he stepped back, and the second scholar stepped forward and clothed the bones with flesh, and blood, and skin, and fur. Then he stepped back, and the third scholar stepped forward, about to breathe the breath of life into the animal, when the fourth man said "Wait! That's a lion! That's a lion you are about to bring to life. It could eat us up! Stop! Think what you're doing!"

"We know what we're doing," said the scholars. "We have studied this all our lives. Don't worry. Just leave everything to us."

"Well, all right," said their friend, "but…could you wait till I climb a tree?"

"Certainly," said the scholars, and they waited till their friend had climbed a convenient tree. Then the third scholar went back to the procedure of breathing the breath of life into the animal. And sure enough, the lion started breathing, opened its eyes, looked at the three scholars, sprang upon them, and ate them up.

After the lion had gone away, the fourth man, the one who wasn't a scholar, climbed down from the tree and made his way back to the village, taking with him no great treasure of gold and jewels, but only his own common sense.

THE HANDSOME PRINCE

ONCE UPON A TIME, a long time ago, in a land far away, there lived a king and a queen who had everything…except children. They waited, and they waited, and at last they had a son. He was a beautiful baby — so beautiful that they called him the Handsome Prince. The king and the queen had no other children after that, and their son was so charming that they gave in to his every whim. So he grew from a beautiful baby, to a spoiled little boy, to an arrogant and self-indulgent young man who was always demanding his own way, and nearly always getting it. People still called him the Handsome Prince, but only out of habit, for he was so very lazy and self-indulgent that it showed in every line of his face and figure.

And so we have the Handsome Prince on the day when our story begins. It began like any other day in the prince's life — he woke up, opened one eye, and instantly his servants rushed to get his breakfast, which they brought to him on a tray carved of solid jade. They set the tray by his bedside, and the prince ate a bountiful breakfast in bed, as he always did. The instant he was finished, the servants whisked away the tray and brought him his shirt, which was made of the finest green silk (for green was the royal color of that kingdom). Then they brought him his pants, which were of exactly the same shade of green. The prince allowed his servants to dress him — he never dressed himself; he hardly knew how to button a button. Then he went downstairs to sit at a table all morning playing checkers with his courtiers. This was his favorite pastime, because they always let him win.

But this day was not to be like any other day in the prince's life, because on this day a soft spring breeze stole into the castle and lured the prince outside — out the gate, down the road, past the lazily turning windmills, and down to the river. It was the first time he had walked so far unattended.

When he got to the river, the prince found the royal sailboat. He head never sailed it himself, but he thought that it, too, would obey his every whim, so he climbed in, untied it, and the boat went drifting down the river. At first the prince drifted past houses and barns and other boats of every description, but at last he came to a place where there were no barns, no houses, and his was the only boat on the river. And it was getting dark, and he was getting hungry. He tried to turn the boat around to make it go home, but he didn't know how. It was all he could do to get the boat to the riverbank and tie it up. He saw that there were no servants there to bring him his supper, and he realized that he would have to find someone who would.

He searched through the boat until he found a lantern, and managed to get it lit. Then he set off across the darkening countryside to see what he could find. At first he saw nothing but grass and sheep, but at last the rays of his lantern fell on a young woman, lying asleep under a tree. "A beautiful princess!" said the prince, for since she was beautiful, he assumed she must be a princess, though she was dressed like any shepherdess. "I will awaken her with a kiss!" But at that moment the young woman woke up. "You're not supposed to wake up until I kiss you," said the prince.

"Whatever are you talking about?" said the young woman. "I wake up whenever I hear a sound, for I must protect my sheep."

"Well, I am going to kiss you anyway," said the prince, "because you are a beautiful girl and I am a handsome prince."

"But I don't want to kiss you! And as for handsome—with that soft white skin and that shiny green suit, you look just like a frog."

"A *frog*? Nonsense!" said the prince, and he kissed her anyway...and the moment he kissed her, he turned into a big, soft, green frog.

So if you ever hear a story about a frog who was really a prince under an enchantment, now you know how he got that way.

The figures look best made from Japanese origami paper. It is square, colored on one side and white on the other. The largest size, about 8 inches square, is easiest to use. Typing paper, gift wrap, or any strong flexible paper may be cut square and used.

PRELIMINARY FOLDS

1. Put paper flat on the table, colored side down.
2. Fold the square in half to a rectangle, crease.

FIGURE 1

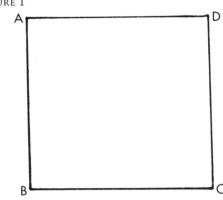

FIGURE 2

3. Fold the rectangle in half to a smaller square, crease.
4. Unfold the folds. Dotted lines show creases.

FIGURE 3

FIGURE 4

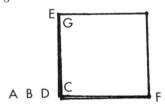

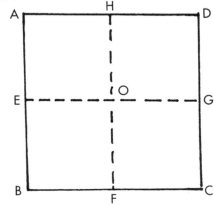

5. Fold corners A, B, C, and D to center O so edges of paper touch creased lines but do not over lap.
6. Turn figure over. Fold corners E, F, G, and H to center O. Do not overlap.
7. Turn figure over. Fold corners I, J, K, and L to center.

THE TRAY

8. Turn figure 7 over.
9. Open out the four little squares (Figure 9a shows square G partly open) so that points E, F, G, and H each rest on corners M, N, P, and Q (Figure 9b), crease.

FIGURE 5

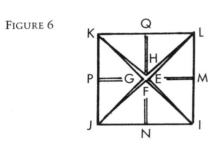

FIGURE 6

FIGURE 7

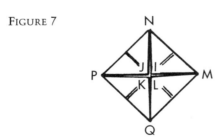

(Figures 8 on will be shown enlarged.)

FIGURE 8

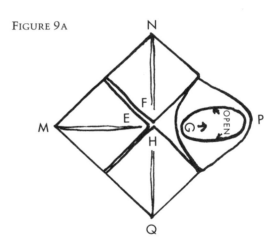

FIGURE 9A

FIGURE 9B

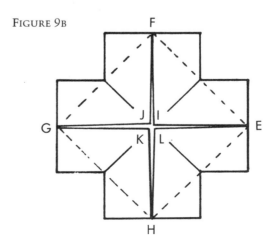

10. Turn over. Raise points I, J, K, and L to make
four triangular legs to use as tray's stand.
11. Turn over.

FIGURE 10

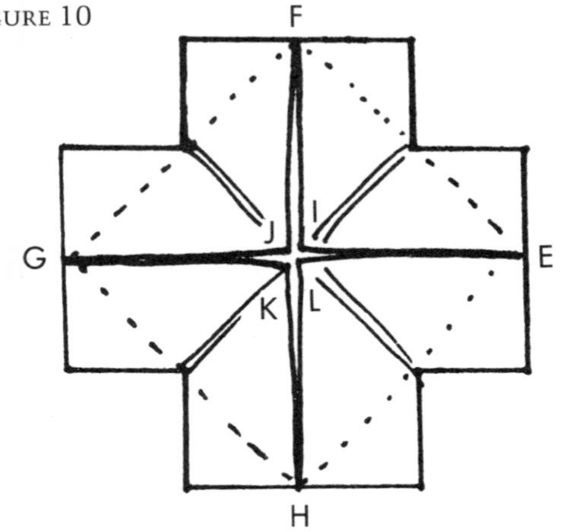

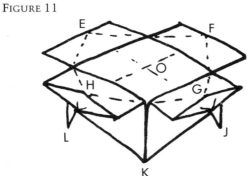

FIGURE 11

Figure 13

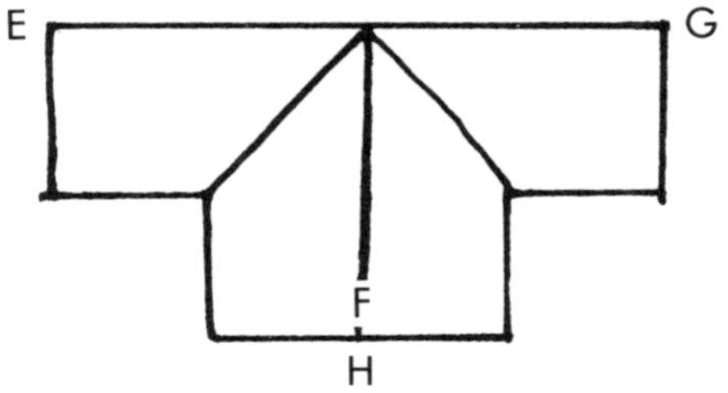

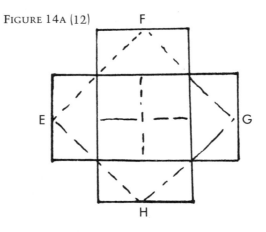

THE PANTS

14. Unfold shirt back to figure 12.
Unfold side flaps, bringing points E
and G back to center O to reform small squares.

FIGURE 14A (12)

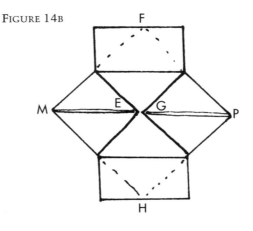

THE SHIRT

12. Fold back the four legs .
13. Fold figure 12 in half (point F over point H).

FIGURE 12

FIGURE 14B

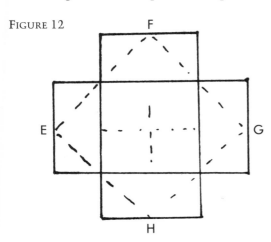

15. Turn figure over.
16. Unfold points I, J, K, and L.
17. Turn figure over.

18. Unfold E and G.
19. Turn over.

FIGURE 15

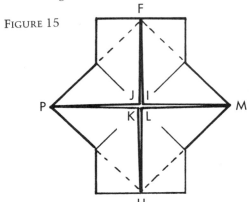

FIGURE 18

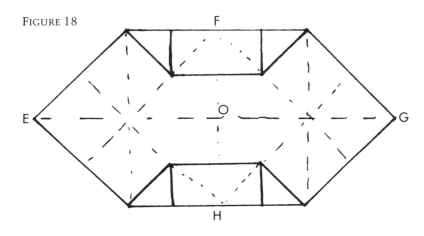

FIGURE 16

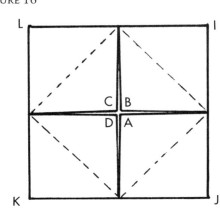

FIGURE 19

FIGURE 17

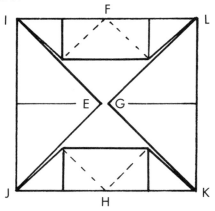

20. Fold points I, J, K, and L along the creases to center O leaving points E and G standing to form legs. Fold legs down.

FIGURE 20

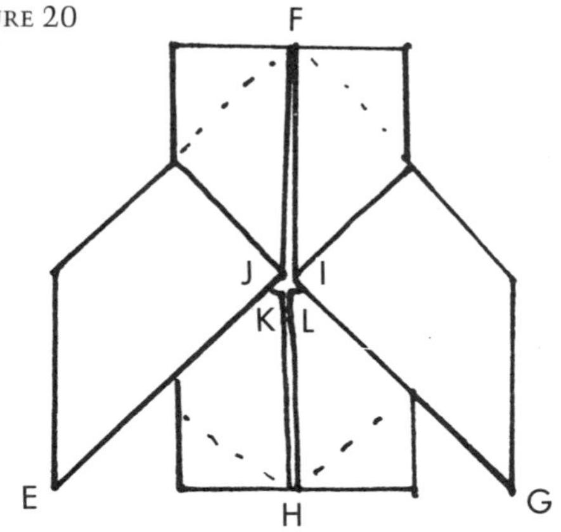

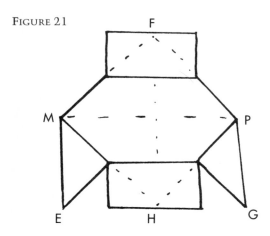

21. Turn figure over.
22. Fold H over on F along the creased line M-P.

FIGURE 21

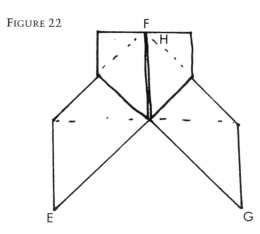

FIGURE 22

The Table

23. Unfold pants back to figure 18.
24. Unfold F and H to center.

FIGURE 23.

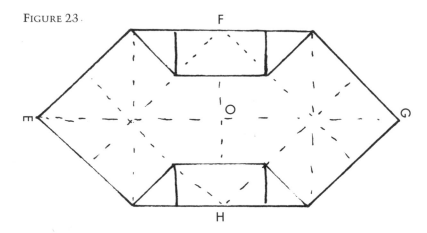

FIGURE 24

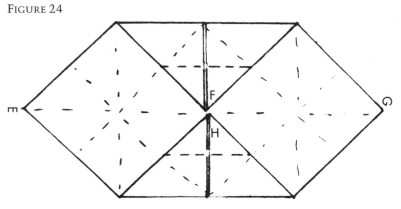

25. Unfold F and H away from center, turn figure over.

26. Bring points I, J, K, and L to center, leaving corners E, F, G and H standing to form four legs. Turn over.

FIGURE 25

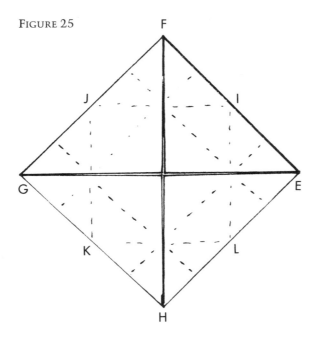

FIGURE 26

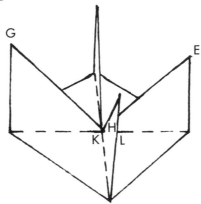

THE WINDMILL

27. Start with figure 26. Bend legs E, F, G, and H down clockwise.

FIGURE 27

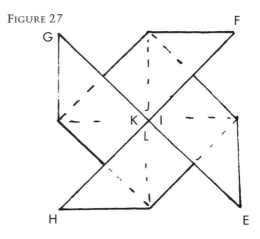

THE SAILBOAT

28. Flip leg E to meet leg F. Flip leg H over, so that points G and H are on one line.

29. Turn over.

FIGURE 28

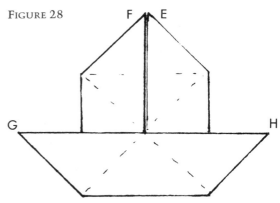

FIGURE 29

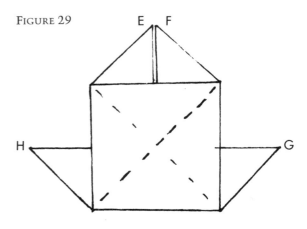

30. Fold E over on G following the crease line.

FIGURE 30

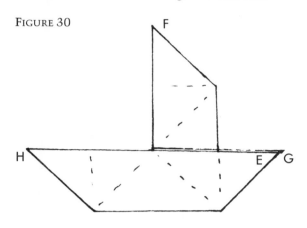

THE LANTERN

31. Unfold the steps back to fugure 25, then follow steps 6 through 8.
32. Open out squares F and H.

FIGURE 32

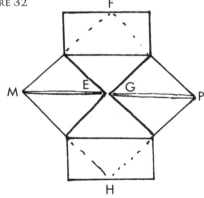

THE FROG

33. Refold F to center.
34. Open out square E, so that two squares next to each other are open to form two eyes.
35. Turn over.

FIGURE 34

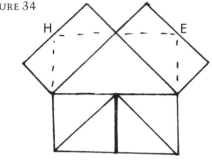

FIGURE 35

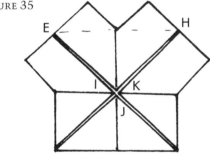

36. Unfold I, J, and K.

FIGURE 36

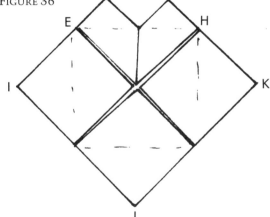

37. Turn over.

FIGURE 37

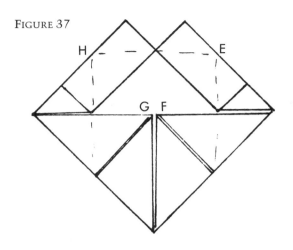

38. Unfold F and G.
39. Turn over. Bring points I, J, and K to center, leaving points F and G standing to form frog's hind legs. Lift flap L to form front of frog.

FIGURE 38

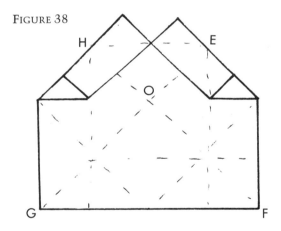

FIGURE 39

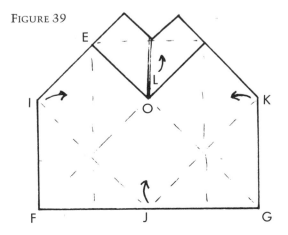

40. Turn over.

FIGURE 40

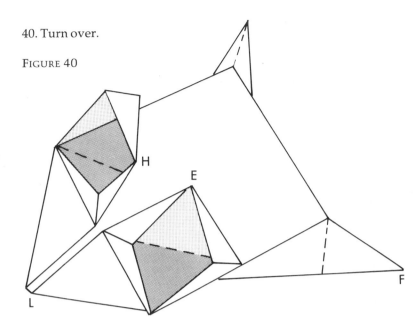

NOTE: If time is short, a group may be taught to make the frog directly from the tray (figure 11) skipping the other figures. Holding the tray between flaps E and H, unfold the other two flaps so points F and G are returned to center O. Pull legs I, J, and k up and out level with the tray top. Unfold F and G to form figure 38, continue as in 38 and 39 above. The front half of the frog is tray, the back half is table.

USING STORIES IN PROGRAMS

STORIES CAN BE TOLD ALMOST anywhere, under almost any circumstances, though I have found that doing a story program in competition with a nearby bagpiper is a losing proposition. At an outdoor, shopping mall, or festival setting, it is good to have a friend or assistant to steer wandering musicians or loud conversations elsewhere. Another story-teller, who can protect you and spell you off as well, is even more useful, as it is usually easier to keep a crowd than to attract one in these circumstances.

Ideally, I like to tell in a fairly quiet but not silent place. I like a barrier behind me so that the audience is not distracted by passers-by, but no barrier defin-ing the limits of the audience area, so people feel free to come and go, and listen while pretending not to. Indoors or out, I try to be facing the light source, so my audience is not squinting up into it. I prefer not to be placed under a clock, as so often happens in school rooms. Whether I stand, perch on a table or stool, sit in a chair, or sit on the floor depends on the size, age and formality of the group, but I try to place myself so everybody can see me, and vice versa. If there are chairs for the audience, I feel best when they are in about third-of-a-circle curves — more informal than straight lines, but not so hard for me to look at as a half-circle or whole circle. There's also something in altering the space to suit myself that feels good.

Circumstances, of course, are rarely ideal. I try to think ahead to avert interruptions — is there some-one who can answer the phone? can we disconnect the intercom announcement system? ask the library clerk to schedule typing for other than storytimes? But the best insurance is to know the story well enough to be able to stop, wait for the fire engines to go by, and pick up the thread again without get-ting lost.

What about interruptions from young audiences? Some of them can be prevented by saying in your introduction, "If you know this story, just smile, and I'll know you know, but let's keep the ending a secret between us." If the interruption is a ques-tion related to the story that can be answered very briefly, I do so. Other questions and comments I try to acknowledge but not answer. It's no use trying to ignore them; the child will just think you didn't hear and will repeat the comment louder. Nod, or say "That's nice," or "I'll tell you later," and go on. Then pick up on it when the story is over. An assistant can help here, too, to take care of needs that can't wait.

Pre-school story time at a library is a special chal-lenge, since many pre-schoolers are not used to lis-tening, or even being, in groups, no matter how well they listen individually at home. For this rea-son, many libraries restrict storytimes to three-year-olds and older. Attendance is often restricted so that the storyteller can reach out and touch a child who is distracting other children. Storytimes for children younger than three can work if the chil-dren are on parents' laps. Stretches, songs, finger-plays, Mother Goose rhymes and conversation can help sustain attention during a program for young children. You can remove a major distraction by asking the children to give you the books they are looking at and any toys they brought, so you can put them up front to be claimed later. Parents can also be a distraction, and librarians may ask them to wait in another part of the library. Some kind of ritual, such as beginning with the same song or fin-gerplay each week, or lighting a storytime candle, serves as a signal that it's time to listen and also pro-vides the security of the familiar. Children like favorite stories repeated from time to time also. It helps to keep a list of what you've done. Though Vardine Moore's helpful *Pre-School Story Hour* (Scarecrow, 1972) is out of print, it is readily avail-able in libraries.

For any age, I like to have a theme for the program. A theme enables me to go from one story to the next in a simple, conversational way, and helps me remember what I'm doing next, but it is not necessary and I don't always have one. A story or song that doesn't fit the theme at first glance may fit well if I change the way I introduce it to point out the connection. This can also give me a fresh approach to the story. I don't generally announce the title of a story before I tell it, especially if the title gives away something better disclosed in the course of the story. I try to remember to give some idea of what's coming up when I begin the program, and to start with a short story so newcomers to story programs will have an idea of what a story is like and a sense of completion right away. Then I might tell a longer story, perhaps one that requires concentration from the listener. Then a stretch, song, or short story for a change of pace, and end with a story that is an attention-keeper, either through suspense, humor, or audience participation. This is not a rule, and will certainly need to be varied at times. If the attention-keeper has a violent ending, or a sad one, it might go better in the middle of the program, or be followed at the end by a short, comforting story or song.

I usually warn the audience if I am going to tell a scary or bloody story; then they can brace themselves, and say "That wasn't so scary" afterwards. And it wasn't so scary, listening in a group, but it might be, thinking about it alone later. Kathryn Windham, who tells ghost stories most convincingly, also passes on a few beliefs about how to keep ghosts away at night. The simplest is to place your shoes with one pointing toward your bed and one pointing away.

People tend to remember liking certain stories at a younger age than they actually did, and consequently try myths, fairy tales, and *Alice in Wonderland* on children too young for them. According to Josephine Gardner, whose little Porpoise Press pamphlet, *How to Tell a Story*, is long out of print, "Children under the age of five years do not need fairy tales. The world is sufficiently wonderful to them." I think some of the objection to violence in fairy tales is a result of assuming that they are for very young children, which they are not. The more complicated fairy tales require an audience much older than five, as do the myths, whose power and strangeness is lost in simplified versions intended for younger children.

Some stories appeal to a wide age range, and come in handy when a teller is faced with a mixed audience of pre-school and older children. I use "The Foolish Frog," "Lazy Jack," "The Lion in the Path," "The Rainhat," "Magic Wings," "Two Donkeys" and "Bye-Bye".

How long should a program be? The youngest and very oldest prefer short programs of short stories; older children I usually tell to for about forty-five minutes; my adult programs are generally one and one-half hours with a break. When I was doing regular pre-school storytimes, I would start at about twenty minutes, lengthening this to around thirty-five minutes as they got used to listening, became familiar with the songs, and as we got to talking together between stories.

Listeners in convalescent homes, aged and infirm, need programs planned especially for them. They are often physically uncomfortable or straining to hear, so each story should be short, perhaps not more than eight minutes. An old familiar tale will reach those who remember but have trouble understanding something new. A story of human foibles or cleverness will amuse those whose infirmities are physical, not mental. A list of stories recommended for adult audiences follows this chapter. As the old are often treated as children and understandably resent this, it is better to start with stories clearly meant for adults, and wait till rapport is established before telling stories that might be perceived as "kid stuff."

Telling stories in rest homes requires commitment on the part of the teller. If you visit once or twice and then stop, you could be one more disappointment to people who may already feel abandoned. The teller also needs the cooperation of those running the home, as an attendant's presence is usually necessary when telling to groups. A sound system and visual aids with stories will help you reach those who have difficulty hearing. Not all the residents will be able to express their appreciation of live entertainment as a relief from constant television; but those who can, make this rather difficult storytelling situation one of the most rewarding ones. And for the teller interested in oral history, the old are a valuable source of stories.

Mark Freeman, who has done storytelling and reading to children in hospitals, recommends two books that children experiencing the difficulty of sleeping in a strange bed can relate to: *Ira Sleeps Over* by Bernard Waber (Houghton, 1972) and the eminently tellable *A Bed Just So* by Jeanne Hardendorff (Scholastic, 1977, o.p.). Scary stories are to be avoided here, but Mark uses transformation stories, like "The Beekeeper and the Bewitched Hare" (from *Thistle and Thyme: Tales and Legends from Scot-*

land, Holt, 1962, o.p.) and *Sylvester and the Magic Pebble* by William Steig (Windmill, 1980, c. 1969) to provide children with a metaphor for the strangeness of their own bodies in casts or with scars and stitches.

As a storyteller, you may or may not be involved in publicizing story programs. If you are, you can find many ideas in Bauer's *Handbook for Storytellers*. If this essential is neglected, your other preparations may be for naught, so it is best to be aware of what publicity is being done for your program, and offer what help you can in the way of snappy descriptions, photographs, story titles.

Sources for Stories to Tell to Adults

Many stories written for adults are too complex to tell, but many stories written or retold for children are of interest to adults. Here are some books published for children and for adults which contain stories appropriate to adult audiences from senior high schools to senior centers. Some stories particularly suited to junior high are indicated by bold face.

In his book *In the Ever After: Fairy Tales and the Second Half of Life* (Chiron, 1989), Allan B. Chinen, a Jungian psychologist, collects and retells fifteen traditional stories with older people as protagonists and analyzes their meaning for continued psychological development in maturity. The well-told stories come from various cultures and the sources he retells from are given.

A good source of personal stories and thoughts about the genre is *A Celebration of American Family Folklore: Tales and Traditions from the Smithsonian Collection*, by Steven J. Zeitlin, Amy J. Kotkin and Holly Cutting Baker (Pantheon, 1982). Most of the stories were collected by folklorists from visitors to the Smithsonian's annual Folklife Festival. The book also includes some fine discussions of family folklore — stories, traditions, sayings, etcetera — and how to collect it. The anecdotes are the kind that will prompt older listeners to say, "That reminds me of a story…"

Lucille and Bren Breneman's *Once Upon a Time: A Storytelling Handbook* (Nelson Hall, 1983) contains a list of "Short Stories for Storytelling," thirty-one stories from short story collections published for adults that lend themselves to oral telling.

Arabian Nights Entertainments. Dover, c.1946. Retold by Andrew Lang.

Babbitt, Natalie. *The Devil's Storybook*. Farrar, 1974. Especially "Perfection" and **"The Power of Speech."**

Babbitt, Natalie. *The Devil's Other Storybook*. Farrar, 1987.

Best-Loved Stories Told at the National Storytelling Festival. National Association for the Preservation and Perpetuation of Storytelling, 1991. "The Woodcutter's Story," others.

Chase, Richard. *American Folk Tales and Songs*. Dover reprint. Especially "Pack Down the Big Chest" and **"Seven Irishmen"** (which can — and should — be told as "Seven Brothers."

Chase, Richard. *Grandfather Tales*. Houghton, 1948. Especially **"Wicked John and the Devil"** and **"Old Dry Frye."**

Courlander, Harold and George Herzog. *The Cow-Tail Switch and Other West African Stories*. Holt, 1947. Especially the title story and **"Talk."**

Courlander, Harold. *The Piece of Fire and Other Haitian Tales*. Harcourt, 1964, o.p. Especially **"Ticoumba and the President."**

Courlander, Harold. *Terrapin's Pot of Sense*. Holt, 1957. Especially "Brer Rabbit's Human Weakness."

Dobie, J. Frank. *Legends of Texas*. Vols. I and II. Pelican, 1975.

Farjeon, Eleanor. *The Little Bookroom*. Godine, 1984. Especially "The Seventh Princess."

Farjeon, Eleanor. *Martin Pippin in the Daisy Field*. Stokes, 1938, o.p. "Elsie Piddock Skips in Her Sleep." Reprinted in Eileen Colwell's *A Storyteller's Choice*, Walck, 1964, o.p.
An old woman is the heroine.

Goss, Linda and Marian E. Barnes, editors. *Talk That Talk: An anthology of African-American storytelling*. Simon & Schuster, 1989.

Ginsburg, Mirra. *The Lazies, Tales of the Peoples of Russia*. Macmillan, 1973, o.p. Especially **"Sheidulla"** and "Two Frogs."

Hearn, Lafcadio. *Kwaidan: Stories and Studies of Strange Things*. C. E. Tuttle, 1971. Especially "Mujina."

Hodges, Margaret, adapter. *The Wave*. Houghton, 1964. From Lafcadio Hearn's *Gleaning in Buddha-fields*.
An old man is the hero.

Housman, Laurence. *The Rat-Catcher's Daughter*. Atheneum, 1974, o.p.

Howe, Irving and Ilana Wiener Howe. *Short Shorts*. Godine, 1982.

Jacobs, Joseph. *English Fairy Tales*. Dover, 1967, c.1898. Especially **"Mr. Fox"** and "Master of All Masters."

Jacobs, Joseph. *More English Fairy Tales*. Dover, 1967, c.1904. Especially "The Peddler of Swaffham."

Kelsey, Alice. *Once the Hodja*. Longmans, 1943, o.p.

Kelsey, Alice. *Once the Mullah*. Longmans, 1954, o.p.

Kennedy, Richard. *Richard Kennedy: Collected Stories*. Harper, 1987.

Kipling, Rudyard. *Just So Stories*. Holt, 1987, c.1902 (many other editions available). Especially "The Cat That Walked By Himself."

Kroeber, Theodora. *The Inland Whale: Nine Stories Retold from California Indian Legends*. University of California Press, 1959.

LeGuin, Ursula. *Buffalo Gals and Other Animal Presences*. ROC Fantasy, 1990. [c. 1987, Capra.]

Lobel, Arnold. *Fables*. Harper, 1980.

Longfellow, Henry W. *Paul Revere's Ride*. Greenwillow, 1985.

Nemirow, Steven, editor. *Coyote's Journal*. Wingbow, 1982.

McHugh, Joe. *Ruff Tales: High Octane Stories from the Ruff Creek General Store*. Catalpa, 1988. **"Meeting Up with a Bear."** Other appropriate stories include a union/ghost story, "The Haunted Wagon."

Minard, Rosemary. *Womenfolk and Fairy Tales*. Houghton, 1975.

Sandburg, Carl. *The Rootabaga Stories*. Harcourt, 1922. Especially "The White Horse Girl and the Blue Wind Boy."

Schimmel, Nancy. *Just Enough to Make a Story*. Sisters' Choice, 1978, 1991. "Lionmakers," "The Tailor," **"The Rainhat"** and **"The Handsome Prince."**

Schimmel, Nancy. *Plum Pudding*. Sisters' Choice Recordings, "The Woodcutter's Story."

Service, Robert. *The Shooting of Dan McGrew. The Cremation of Sam McGee*. Godine, 1988.

Serwer, Blanche. *Let's Steal the Moon: Jewish Tales, Ancient and Recent*. Shapolsky, 1987, c.1970. Especially "Did the Tailor Have a Nightmare?"

Shah, Idries. *Tales of the Dervishes*. Dutton, 1970.

Singer, Isaac B. *The Fearsome Inn*. Macmillan, 1984.

Smith, Jimmy Neil. *Homespun: Tales from American's Favorite Storytellers*. Crown, 1988.

Stockton, Frank. *Lady or the Tiger & Other Stories*. Airmont, 1968.

Tashjian, Virginia. *Juba This and Juba That: Story Hour Stretches for Large or Small Groups*. Little, Brown, 1966. **"The Yellow Ribbon."**

Twain, Mark. *The Jumping Frog and Other Stories*. Peter Pauper, 1985.

Van der Post, Laurens. *Patterns of Renewal*. Pendle Hill, 1962. Especially pp. 4-5 for the story about the basket.

Viorst, Judith. *Alexander and the Terrible, Horrible, No Good, Very Bad Day*. Atheneum, 1972.

Wolkstein, Diane. *The Magic Orange Tree and Other Haitian Folktales*. Knopf, 1987. Especially **"Owl."**

Yamaguchi, Marianne. *The Sea of Gold and Other Tales from Japan*. Creative Arts, 1988. "The Wise Old Woman."

Yolen, Jane. *Dream Weaver*. Putnam, 1989. Especially **"The Cat Bride."**

Zemach, Harve. *A Penny a Look: An Old Story Retold*. Farrar, 1971.

Zipes, Jack. *Don't Bet on the Prince*. Methuen, 1986. Especially "Petronella" by Jay Williams, which is also in Jay Williams' *The Practical Princess and Other Liberating Fairy Tales* (o.p.) and was published separately as a picture book (o.p.).

USING STORIES IN SCHOOL AND AT HOME

MOST STORYTELLING IS NOT DONE in story programs. It is used to put children to sleep, pass along the family history, recount the day over dinner. Storytelling precedes radios and tape players as a way to pass the time during repetitive work. Speakers and teachers illustrate points and enliven talks with stories, singers introduce songs with stories. Leo Rosten, in his introduction to his dictionary, *The Joys of Yiddish* (McGraw-Hill, 1968), says:

"I have used a story, joke, or anecdote in the main body of this lexicon to illustrate the meaning of a word, whenever possible. Since this is highly unorthodox in lexicography, a brief for the defense may be in order.

"I consider the story, the anecdote, the joke, a teaching instrument of unique efficacy. A joke is a structured, compact narrative that makes a point with power, generally by surprise. A good story is exceedingly hard for anyone to forget. It is therefore an excellent pedagogic peg on which to hang a point. Those who do not use stories when they try to explain or communicate are either inept at telling them or blindly forfeit a tool of great utility."

Librarians and teachers need not restrict their use of storytelling to storytime. Librarians can use stories in class visits where the primary purpose is to give book talks or library instruction, and in talks to teachers, community organizations, et cetera, to break the ice, make a point, encourage storytelling, or promote support of library programs. Your listeners will feel they have shared an experience with you (the events of the story) and will be more likely to talk to you when they come to the library.

Teachers and parents can use stories to introduce new subjects, fill waiting time, and give examples of conflicts similar to ones arising in school or home, which may encourage discussion of things otherwise hard to talk about calmly. Telling any story the teller cares about, especially one about the teller's childhood, has the potential of creating a bond between teller and listener. It takes a great leap of faith for children to believe that the world existed before they were born, but it is possible for parents, grandparents and teachers to interest them in tales of the teller's youth if they are stories about the times the teller was scared or surprised or embarrassed or up to no good. Grandparents and aunts and uncles can tell stories on parents that the parents wouldn't tell themselves. All this gives children a greater sense of belonging in their own family or of personal acquaintance with their teacher, and it also opens their imagination to those other stories of former times that we call history.

When you tell stories about your own life, it can be hard to figure out where each story begins and ends. With kids, you have to cut to the chase pretty quickly. If you tell often, you can build the cast of characters (your parents and siblings, childhood friends, teachers) gradually, and not have to do so much explaining each time before you get to the action. Take the time to remember the people and places vividly so the stories will sound fresh. Looking at snapshots, if you have them, can help. If you can, tell how the incident changed you — your understanding of someone, your aspirations, whatever. Or say how looking back on the incident seems different from your feeling at the time. Connect the story to the you they know. I've put down a few more of my thoughts on family storytelling in "Telling Stories to Your Kids" in the summer 1991 issue of *Whole Earth Review* (pp.68-69). This issue of WER also contains several other articles on storytelling. *Children Tell Stories* by Martha Hamilton and Mitch Weiss has a chapter on helping children develop family and personal experience stories for telling.

Anne Pellowski's *Family Storytelling Handbook: How to Use Stories, Anecdotes, Rhymes, Handkerchiefs, Paper, and Other Objects to Enrich Your Family Tradi-

tions includes many stories best told in an intimate setting as well as advice on when, where and how to bring stories into family life. In *Awakening the Hidden Storyteller: How to Build a Storytelling Tradition in Your Family* (Shambhala, 1991), Robin Moore tells how to use simple rituals and guided meditations to incorporate storytelling, listening and storymaking into family life. This title is available as a book or as a set of tapes.

Children have their own folklore—counting-out rhymes, skip-rope rhymes, taunts and singing games—which they have handed down for hundreds of years without adult assistance. "The games are a form of lore, a tradition which in certain aspects reaches back into tribal origins...we adults—teachers especially—watching children at their games, tend to think that because children are new, we ourselves have a great deal to offer. We neglect to observe that we are competing with a durable and compelling tradition."[1]

It might make sense for children to begin their study of folklore with their own lore, rather than with the stories of Paul Bunyan or Pecos Bill (for a folklorist's entertaining and informative view of the Paul Bunyan tales, see Richard Dorson's *America in Legend, Folklore from the Colonial Period to the Present*, Pantheon, 1973, pp.168-170).

Shake It to the One That You Love Best : Play Songs and Lullabies from Black Musical Traditions by Cheryl Warren Mattox (Warren-Mattox Productions, distributed by JTG of Nashville, 1989) and other collections of children's lore can be used, not to teach the games and rhymes to children, who already know them, but to draw their attention to local variations, so they will begin to grasp the notion that there are many "right" versions of folklore. It should then be easier for them to accept versions of folktales different from the ones they are used to. They may even be inspired to make their own collection by taping or writing down the rhymes they know and asking friends, parents, teachers for their versions.

To deepen our own appreciation of this rich tradition that surrounds those of us who work with children and that can call up our own childhood memories, there are several excellent studies of the history, meaning and function of children's games and rhymes:

Step It Down: Games, Plays, Songs, and Stories from the Afro-American Heritage by Bessie Jones and Bess Lomax Hawes (U. of Georgia Press, 1987, c. 1972)

One Potato, Two Potato...The Secret Education of American Children by Mary and Herbert Knapp (Norton, 1976)

The Lore and Language of Schoolchildren by Iona and Peter Opie (Oxford U. Press, 1987, c. 1959)

Another approach to using storytelling in education has been developed by Vivian Gussin Paley, a sharply observing and self-aware teacher who describes her work in *The Boy Who Would Be a Helicopter: The Uses of Storytelling in the Classroom* (Harvard U. Press, 1990). She writes down stories her pre-school children tell her and has the group act them out later under the direction of the story's creator. She assumes this way of learning would be available to any child—I think her practice of reading two books aloud to the class every day and reading to individual children on request may have something to do with her students' skill.

Lynn Landor describes a parallel program for school-age children in her book, *Children's Own Stories: A Literature-Based Language Arts Program, Grades k-4.* (Zellerbach Family Fund, 1990.) Students dictate their own stories—real and imaginary—to a teacher, aide, or volunteer who records them verbatim without comment or correction (the students can make corrections when the story is read back to them). Through these weekly small-group sessions the students' storymaking improves, and they learn about each other by listening to and reading (when offered) each other's stories.

Tall tales can also be used to improve students' writing skills. They are full of simile and metaphor, and telling or reading them to a class can inspire students to create some exaggerated similes and metaphors of their own (according to a "Curriculum Booster" on page 31 of the March issue of *Learning86*).

Several story collections have come out recently that include activities to go with each story:

> Caduto, Michael J. and Joseph Bruchac. *Keepers of the Earth: Native American Stories and Environmental Activities for Children.* Fulcrum, 1988.
>
> Sierra, Judy, Kaminski, Robert. *Twice upon a Time: Stories to Tell, Retell, Act Out, and Write About.* Wilson, 1989.
>
> *Spinning Tales — Weaving Hope: Stories of Peace, Justice and the Environment.* New Society, 1991.

I never met a storyteller who doubted the value of his or her efforts. We all know in our bones that enjoyment of stories motivates kids to read, and the practice in imagining pictures to go with the stories helps them to make the transition from picture books to books without pictures. We are convinced that listening to stories "develops the imagination," though we wonder how we can test that, or even describe the process. We are not surprised when we read Tim Jennings' account[2] of winning the attention of a group of twelve-year-old nonreaders by telling folktales, when all his attempts to get them to listen to him read stories aloud had failed. But sometimes we need to convince others, if storytelling is to be budgeted, or even allowed.

In 1977 Garth H. Brown studied the relation of a child's "sense of story" (the sense of how a story should progress logically, which helps the child predict *what* is likely to be stated on the printed page and *how* it might be written) to the child's reading abilty, and concluded: "The inability to develop reading much beyond a plodding and tedious almost word by word performance, appears related to difficulty in 'moving into' the language of story…. It may be true, too, that the extent of the child's sense of story influences comprehension [comprehension being defined as the ability to retell a story one has read]…. Listening to stories being told or read aloud throughout the elementary school must be helpful and seems crucial to reading and writing growth."[3]

Donald Davis' anecdotal account of his experience in telling folktales to fourth and fifth graders[4] seems to support Brown's ideas. Davis told several stories in one very simple folk form, then a week later told several in a slightly more complex form, and so on. After sixteen sessions, he found that the students spontaneously organized their own stories into these forms without having been taught to, except by example. If you want to try this, Chapter Two in Norma Livo's book, *Storytelling: Process and Practice* (Libraries Unlimited, 1986) would be helpful, as it lists stories by form: cumulative stories of various types, event-repeat stories, chronicle pattern tales (held together by their logical sequence of events) and the embedded-story form (story within a frame story).

While anecdotal evidence such as Davis' and Jennings' is the kind storytellers themselves are most likely to take seriously, there have been few "scientific" studies of the effects of telling, and fewer rigorous ones with clear results that would convince library and school boards of the worth of story programs.

To test the helpfulness of storytelling in developing comprehension, Catharine Farrell conducted a study of the effects of storytelling by teachers and professional storytellers in two kindergartens and two first grades in 1981-1982. Students who heard many stories during the school year showed more improvement in their ability to retell a story they heard, and to make up original story elements to extend the story, than did students in the control classes not exposed to storytelling.[5]

Improving students' ability "to make up original story elements" may be a testable instance of "developing the imagination." The same effect may be showing up in a study by Anthony Amato and others in 1973,[6] in which neither storytelling nor creative dramatics had any measurable effects on reading interest or reading ability of children, but the group attending storytelling increased scores on a test of creativity.

Two articles from *Psychology Today,* not on storytelling but on children's ability to daydream and engage in imaginative play, may also provide ammunition for the teacher trying to make room for fairy tales in the curriculum. Both Joan Freyberg[7] and, at greater length, Mary Ann Spencer Pulaski[8] cite studies showing that children who fantasize well can sit still longer, dissipate aggressive feelings through fantasy, and think more creatively. The authors also give techniques for encouraging imaginative play among children.

Similar results were obtained in an experiment conducted more recently by William Crain[9] and others. One of the authors had noticed that fairy tales seemed to have a calming effect on children when she told them at summer camp. The authors reasoned that if Bettelheim is correct in his theory that the symbolic language of fairy tales enables children to apply a story to their own private concerns and get reassurance, then children after hearing fairy tales might become introspective and composed. In fact, in two experiments (one with 9- to 11-year-olds and one with 6-year-olds), small groups of children did play more quietly, and were more solitary and less distractable, after hearing a fairy tale, than after hearing an equally violent but trivial story or watching a cartoon. They seemed to independent observers to be absorbed in their own thoughts.

Further studies and much anecdotal evidence for the educational value of storytelling (and particularly of students telling stories as well as hearing them) can be found in *Children Tell Stories: A Teaching Guide*. The authors, Martha Hamilton and Mitch Weiss, have done such a good job of updating this section of my book that rather than duplicate their efforts I simply refer you to the first chapter of their excellent book.[10]

[1]Dennison, George. *The Lives of Children: The Story of the First Street School*. Random, 1970, p. 202.

[2]Jennings, Tim. "Storytelling — A Nonliterate Approach to Reading," *Learning Magazine* April/May 1981, pp. 48-52. Reprinted in *Yarnspinner* Nov. 1981.

[3]Brown, Garth H. "Development of Story in Children's Reading and Writing," *Theory into Practice* Dec 1977, pp. 357-361.

[4]Davis, Donald D. "Storytelling and Comprehension Skills — A Classroom Experiment," *Yarnspinner* Dec. 1982, pp. 1-2, reprinted in *Stories: A Western Storytelling Newsletter* Winter 1988.

[5]Farrell, Catharine Horne and Denise D. Nessel. *Effects of Storytelling: An Ancient Art for Modern Classrooms*. Word Weaving, P. O. Box 5646, San Francisco, CA 94101. 27 p.

[6]Amato, Anthony, Elsie Ziegler and Robert Evans. "The Effectiveness of Creative Dramatics and Storytelling in a Library Setting," *The Journal of Educational Research* Dec 1973, pp. 161+.

[7]Freyberg, Joan T. "Hold High the Cardboard Sword," *Psychology Today* Febr. 1975, pp. 63-64.

[8]Pulaski, Mary Ann Spencer. "The Rich Rewards of Make Believe," *Psychology Today* Jan. 1974, pp. 68-74.

[9]Crain, William C., Esterina D'Alessio, Brenda McIntyre, and Leslee Smoke. "The Impact of Hearing a Fairy Tale on Childrens Immediate Behavior," *The Journal of Genetic Psychology* Sept. 1983, pp. 9-17.

[10]Hamilton, Martha and Mitch Weiss. *Children Tell Stories: A Teaching Guide*. Richard C. Owen Publishers, P. O. Box 585, Katonah, NY 10536.

ACTIVE HEROINES IN FOLKTALES

IN MOST FAMILIAR FOLK TALES with female protagonists, the woman or girl plays a passive role, waiting to be rescued or, at most, helping her male rescuer by her special knowledge of her captor. Women with power tend to have secondary roles: wicked stepmother, fairy godmother. Some folk tales in which the central female character takes an active, positive role are listed here. In three of the stories, "Umai," "The Wood Fairy" and "The Sweet Porridge," there are no male characters.

In this index to women taking under-represented roles in traditional stories found in collections for children, the annotations are mostly descriptive. Political or literary analysis is left to you, as is the selection of stories you find both non-sexist and good for telling. The collections of folktales for adults I leave to someone else to search, mentioning only *The Old Wives' Fairy Tale Book* edited by Angela Carter for the Pantheon Fairy Tale and Folklore Library (1990). However, most of the stories listed here can be told to adults.

Since this list was first compiled, several books of folktales with active heroines have appeared, and one, *The Skull in the Snow* by Toni McCarty, has come into and gone out of print. The first to appear, Rosemary Minard's *Womenfolk and Fairy Tales* (Houghton, 1975) is still readily available in libraries and stores, and is an indispensable resource for any storyteller. Ethel Johnston Phelps has edited two collections, *Tatterhood and Other Tales* (Feminist Press, 1978) and *The Maid of the North, Feminist Folk Tales from Around the World* (Holt, 1981). She does more cleaning up of sexist tales than I am comfortable with—I want the tales I tell to represent a tradition of uppity women. I will change sexist language or minor incidents, but not plots or characters. Jack Zipes has collected some non-traditional feminist fairy tales in *Don't Bet on the Prince: Contemporary Feminist Fairy Tales in North America and England* (Methuen, 1986). None of the stories from these five books are annotated here; all are worth looking at. Margaret Read MacDonald has listed some good stories about women and girls in her *Storyteller's Sourcebook*. Some likely numbers to look under are H506.12, H551.0.1 through H561.1.2, and H582.1.1. *Stories—A List of Stories to Tell and Read Aloud*, eighth edition (New York Public Library, 1990) has a number of stories listed under "Heroines" in the index. Both traditional and non-traditional stories are included.

If you know of other stories in folk tale collections for children (or separately published for children) that seem to belong on this Active Heroines list, please send descriptions and sources for the stories to Sisters' Choice, 1639 Channing Way, Berkeley, CA 94703.

***

Ashpet, in *Grandfather Tales* by Richard Chase. Houghton, 1948.
A Cinderella variant in which Ashpet is a hired hand, *earns* the grannylady's magic help, shucks the shoe on purpose, and generally takes things into her own hands. Appalachian.

Atalanta, in *Free to Be...You and Me* by Marlo Thomas. McGraw, 1974.
A modern retelling of the myth, in which Atalanta and Young John tie in the race and become friends. There are also traditional versions in which Atalanta becomes an athlete because her father wanted a son, and it is only with the help of love that any man can win a race against her.

Baba Yaga, in *Old Peter's Russian Tales* by Arthur Ransome. Viking, 1975.
The little girl sent to the witch's house uses thoughtfully everything she finds on the way, and thus makes her escape.

The Barber's Clever Wife, in *Fools and Funny Fellows* by Phyllis Fenner. Knopf, 1947, o.p.
She dupes a pack of thieves on four occasions and finally bites off the tip of their captain's tongue. From *Tales of the Punjab*.

The Beggar in the Blanket, in *The Beggar in the Blanket and Other Vietnamese Tales* by Gail B. Graham. Dial, 1970.
A woman's audacious plan convinces her husband that his poor brother is worth more to him than his rich friends.

Bimwili and the Zimwi, retold by Verna Aardema. Dial, 1985.
Playing at the ocean with her sisters, a girl makes up a song about a seashell. On their way home she remembers her shell, and returns for it alone. When captured by a loathsome ogre, the girl uses a variation on her song to signal for help. Tanzania.

The Black Bull of Norroway, in *More English Fairy Tales* by Joseph Jacobs. Dover, 1967.
Three sisters go out to seek their fortunes; the third rides the black bull and rescues her true love from an evil spell.

Boadicea...The Warrior Queen, in *The World's Great Stories: 55 Legends That Live Forever* by Louis Untermeyer. Lippincott, 1964.
The legend of England's ancient heroine.

The Brave Woman and the Flying Head, in *Iroquois Stories: Heroes and Heroines, Monsters and Magic* by Joseph Bruchac. Crossing, 1985. Also in *Children Tell Stories* by Martha Hamilton and Mitch Weiss. Richard C. Owen, 1990.
A quick-thinking woman saves herself and her small child from the hungry monster.

The Clever Wife, in *Sweet and Sour: Tales from China* by Carole Kendall and Yao-wen Li. Houghton Mifflin, c. 1979.
Fu–Hsing boasts of his wife's cleverness, the Magistrate sets her tasks, and she solves them by turning them back on him.

The Dragon's Revenge, in *Magic Animals of Japan* by Davis Pratt. Parnassus, 1967.
A young man breaks his promise to the woman who loves him; she turns into a dragon and burns him to a crisp.

The Fairy Frog, in *Black Fairy Tales* by Terry Berger. Macmillan, 1974.
Tombi-Ende is buried alive by her jealous sisters, but she keeps crying out, "I am Tombe-Ende, I am not dead, I am alive like one of you," and an enchanted frog hears her and saves her.

The Farmer's Wife and the Tiger, in *The Magic Umbrella and Other Stories for Telling* compiled by Eileen Colwell. David McCay, 1976, o.p.
The tiger demands the farmer's bullocks. The farmer promises his wife's milk cow instead. The wife tricks the tiger out of

both. As retold by Ikram Chugtai in *Folktales from Asia*, Cultural Center for UNESCO. Pakistan.

The Five Eggs, in *Ride with the Sun: An Anthology of Folk Tales and Stories from the United Nations* by Harold Courlander. McGraw-Hill, 1955, o.p.
Juan begs money for five eggs. Juanica cooks them. Each stubbornly claims the right to eat three. Juanica says she'll die, Juan says go ahead, and the grave is dug before she gives in. But when they get home, she eats three eggs. From *Stories from the Americas,* collected and translated by Frank Henius. Ecuador, probably of European origin.

Flossie and the Fox, by Patricia McKissack. Dial, 1986.
The neighbors' hen house has been cleaned out by a fox, so Flossie Finley is taking them a basket of eggs. When an arrogant old fox chats her up along the way, this self-possessed African-American girl uses her quick wit to drive him to distraction. Author's adaptation of a family story.

A Fox Who Was Too Sly, in *Magic Animals of Japan* by Davis Pratt. Parnassus, 1967.
The fox tries to trick an old woman but she tricks—and cooks—him.

The Gay Goss-hawk, in *Heather and Broom: Tales of the Scottish Highlands* by Sorche Nic Leodhas. Holt, 1960, o.p.
An English lady, prevented by her father from marrying her Scottish laird, carries out a bold plan to rejoin her true love. Retold from a ballad.

The Ghost's Bride, in *The Rainbow People* by Laurence Yep. Harper Collins, 1989.
A brave and clever mother saves her daughter from being the bride of a ghost. China.

The Girl Who Overpowered the Moon, in *The Man in the Moon: Sky Tales from Many Lands* by Alta Jablow and Carl Withers. Holt, 1969, o.p.
A Chuckchee tale in which a reindeer herder is pursued by the moon. She keeps tricking the moon until he is exhausted and promises to give her people light at night and to measure the year for them. Siberia.

The Goblin's Giggle, in *The Goblin's Giggle and Other Stories* by Molly Garret Bang. Scribners, 1973.

A bride stolen away by goblins is rescued by her mother and a nun. When the goblins drink the river to catch them, they escape by making the goblins laugh. Japan.

The Husband Who Was to Mind the House, in *East of the Sun and West of the Moon* by P. C. Asbjornsen. Dover, 1970, o.p. Also in *Time for Fairy Tales, Old and New* by May Hill Arbuthnot.
A farmer finds that his wife's work is not so easy as he thinks. Norway.

I'm Tipingee, She's Tipingee, We're Tipingee Too, in *The Magic Orange Tree and Other Haitian Folktales* by Diane Wolkstein. Knopf, 1978.
Tipingee organizes her friends to wear red like her, so the old man who has come to take her away won't be able to pick her out.

The King's True Children, in *The Beautiful Blue Jay and Other Tales of India* by John W. Spellman. Little, Brown, 1967, o.p.
Jealous older wives send the youngest queen's two children down the river, where they are rescued and raised by a fisherman and his wife. When grown, the brother follows a quest to a sacred spring, but looks back and is taken by demons. His sister sees that the milk he left has turned blood red and goes to rescue him. She succeeds, and her fame brings a reunion with their birth parents.

The Lad in Search of a Fortune, in *Cap o' Rushes and Other Folk Tales* by Winifred Finlay. Harvey, 1974, o.p.
A farm lad sets out to find a rich man's daughter and rescue her, but is himself rescued by a wise country lass instead.

The Legend of Bluebonnet, retold by Tomie de Paola. Putnam, 1983.
The Great Spirits told the Comanche People to sacrifice their most precious possession to end a drought that had killed many, including the parents of one little girl. When the little girl sacrificed a doll made for her by her mother, the Spirits covered the hillsides with bluebonnets and ended the drought. Texas legend.

A Legend of Knockmany, in *Celtic Fairy Tales* by Joseph Jacobs. Dover, 1968.
Fin M'Coul is afraid to fight Cuhullin, a bigger giant, so Fin's wife, Oonagh, tricks Cuhullin. Ireland.

The Lion's Whiskers, in *The Lion's Whiskers, Tales of High Africa* by Brent Ashabranner and Russell Davis. Little, Brown, 1959, o.p.
A woman tames a lion in order to win the love of her little stepson. An antidote to all those bad-stepmother stories and a hint about why they exist. Ethiopia.

The Little Daughter of the Snow, in *Old Peter's Russian Tales* by Arthur Ransome. Viking, 1975.
For once it is a daughter, not a son, who is longed for. The girl the old couple make out of snow is active and independent.

The Little Porridge Pot, in *Children Tell Stories* by Martha Hamilton and Mitch Weiss. Richard C. Owen, 1990. In *More Tales from Grimm* by Wanda Gág as "The Sweet Porridge." Coward-McCann, 1947, o.p.
A wise woman gives a poor girl a magic pot. Her mother forgets the words that make it stop producing porridge, and the town is inundated before the girl arrives to stop it. Germany.

Lon Po Po: A Red Riding Hood Story from China, retold by Ed Young. Philomel, 1989.
A girl uses her wits to kill a wolf dressed up as Po Po, her grandmother. The author's dedication thanks "the wolves of the world for lending their good name as a tangible symbol of our darkness.".

The Magic Wings: A Tale from China, retold by Diane Wolkstein.Dutton, 1983.
The goose girl is determined to grow wings, and after all the women in the country become involved, she does. Also in *Joining In*, compiled by Teresa Miller (Yellow Moon, 1988) with instructions from Diane on doing it as a participation story.

Mary Culhane and the Dead Man, in *The Goblin's Giggle and Other Stories* by Molly Garret Bang. Scribners, 1973.
Mary keeps her wits about her even under the power of a dead man, and wins three pots of gold. Ireland.

Mirandy and Brother Wind, by Patricia McKissack. Knopf, 1988.
A turn-of-the-century African-American girl is set on dancing with magical, high-steppin' Brother Wind at the Junior Cake-walk contest. After confiding her plan to catch the wind to the clumsiest boy in town, she sees there's more than one way the wind's magic can help her. Author's adaptation of a family story.

The Moon Princess, in *The Beautiful Blue Jay and Other Tales of India* by John W. Spellman. Little, Brown, 1967, o.p.
Princess Radha rejects all her suitors; they are vain or stingy or talk about food all the time. She wishes for a husband as beautiful as the moon. When Prince Moon's emmisary comes for her, her grandfather argues with him and the little man starts to pull him up to the moon. Radha goes to his rescue and they all end up on the moon, perfectly happy.

The Moon's Escape, in *Once in the First Times, Folk Tales from the Philippines* by Elizabeth Hough Sechrist. MacRae Smith, 1969, o.p.
A princess fights a giant crab who wants to eat the moon.

Mufaro's Beautiful Daughters, by John Steptoe. Lothrop, 1987.
A snake is well treated by a young African woman who knows he is good for her garden. He turns out to be a handsome prince.

Mutsmag, in *Grandfather Tales* by Richard Chase. Houghton, 1948.
An Appalachian tale similar to "Mollie Whuppie" in which a girl steals a giant's treasure, but Mutsmag wins gold, not husbands.

A New Year's Story, in *Tales from a Taiwan Kitchen* by Cora Cheney. Dodd, Mead, 1976, o.p.
The young widow Teng saves her child from the terrible dragon ghost; a legend that explains New Year's customs.

The Nixie of the Mill Pond, in *Fairy Tales* by Jacob Grimm and Wilhelm Grimm. Various editions.
A brave wife rescues her captive husband with the aid of a wisewoman. Germany.

Odilia and Aldaric, in *The Giant at the Ford And Other Legends of the Saints* by Ursula Synge. Atheneum, 1980, o.p. Also available on Milbre Burch's cassette, *Saints and Other Sinners* (Kind Crone).
A warrior rejects his blind daughter and she is raised in a convent. At baptism she regains her sight. Then begins a contest of wills between equally stubborn father and daughter. Alsace. ·

The Old Jar, in *The Rainbow People* by Laurence Yep. Harper Collins, 1989.
An old woman hangs onto an old jar despite difficulties and seemingly better offers, and the jar supplies her with rice for the rest of her life. China.

The Origin of the Camlet Flower, in *Ride with the Sun: An Anthology of Folk Tales and Stories from the United Nations* by Harold Courlander. McGraw-Hill, 1955.
Retold from *Poesias y Leyendas Para los Niños*, by Fernan Silva Valdes.
A white girl drowns while trying to save an Indian child. The Indians bring a message from their god that the girl will live on as a water-flower blue as the girls eyes, and it is so. Uruguay.

The People Who Hugged the Trees: An Environmental Folk Tale, adapted by Deborah Lee Rose. Roberts Rinehart, 1990.
Amrita loves the trees that protect her desert village from sandstorms. When a ruler orders the woods cut, she runs to hug her favorite tree and the other villagers do the same. The ruler is adamant until a sandstorm comes and he sees that the trees are more useful as trees than as a fort. India.

Princess Maring, the Huntress, in *Folk Tales from the Philippines* by Dorothy Lewis Robertson. Dodd, 1971, o.p.
The princess falls in love with her father's enemy while hunting.

The Prisoner, in *The Arbuthnot Anthology of Children's Literature* by May Hill Arbuthnot. 3rd ed. Scott Foresman, 1971, o.p.
A huge fish swallows Rangi when she refuses to marry him. She cuts her way out through the thin flesh of his throat, which is why all fish have gills today. Rarotonga.

Savitri and the Lord of the Dead, in *The Buried Moon and Other Stories* by Molly Bang. Scribners, 1977, o.p.
Savitri, knowing that her husband will die, fasts and meditates. When the Lord of the Dead comes, she can see him, and by her wisdom and cleverness forces him to give back her husband. Also in *Homespun: Tales from America's Favorite Storytellers* as retold by Laura Simms (edited by Jimmy Neil Smith for Crown, 1988).

The Serpent-Slayer, in *Sweet and Sour: Tales from China* by Carol Kendall and Yao-wen Li. Houghton Mifflin, c. 1979.
Li Chi lures the maiden-eating serpent with rice-balls; it scalds itself in the boiling honey-syrup and she slays it.

The Skull, in *The Book of Ghosts and Goblins* by Ruth Manning-Sanders. Dutton, 1973, o.p.
An orphan girl de-haunts and wins a castle by defending a skull from the skeleton that wants to steal it. I prefer to leave the little girl with the castle, playmates and servants she has won from the skeleton. She doesn't need—and the story doesn't need—the promise of a prince later. Tyrolian.

The Slaying of the Sea-Serpent, in *Animal Folktales Around the World* by Kathleen Arnott. Walck, 1971, o.p.
Tokoyo's father is banished for an affront to the Mikado. She fails to find him, so offers to replace a weeping maiden as the annual sacrifice to the sea-serpent. She kills the serpent, finds near it a long-lost statue of the Mikado, and restores her father to favor. Japan.

Slue-Foot Sue and Pecos Bill, in *Larger Than Life: John Henry and Other Tall Tales* by Robert San Souci. Doubleday, 1991.
Slue-Foot Sue rides a giant catfish, but when she tries wearing a bustle she gets into trouble.

Spin, Weave, Wear, in *Heather and Broom: Tales of the Scottish Highlands* by Sorche Nic Leodhas. Holt, 1960, o.p.
This starts like Rumpelstiltskin, but the lass pays in advance for the magic, and strikes a better bargain.

The Squire's Bride, in *Children Tell Stories* by Martha Hamilton and Mitch Weiss. Richard C. Owen, 1990. Also in *Norwegian Folk Tales* by Peter Asbjornsen. Pantheon, 1982. Also published separately, o.p.
The wealthy squire won't take "No!" for an answer, so the farmer's daughter makes him look ridiculous. The *Children Tell Stories* version leaves out the agist aspect.

The Story of Oskus-ool and His Wise Wife, in *How the Moolah Was Taught a Lesson and Other Tales from Russia* by Estelle Titiev and Lila Pargment. Dial, 1976.
Oskus-ool wins wealth and a wife from the old wolf. The wife's beauty draws the envy of the Khan's son, but her wisdom and knowledge of magic protect her. Tuvin.

Strega Nona: An Old Tale, retold by Tomie de Paola. Simon & Schuster, c. 1975.
The good witch's apprentice uses the forbidden pot and inundates the town with pasta. The townspeople want to string him up, but Strega Nona says "Let the punishment fit the crime," and makes him eat all the pasta. Italy.

The Talking Eggs, retold by Robert San Souci. Dial, 1989.
The sister who shows neither fear nor amusement at the old woman's magic is rewarded. African-American.

Tamlane, in *More English Fairy Tales* by Joseph Jacobs. Dover, 1967.
Burd Janet rescues Tamlane from the fairies by holding him as they change him into one frightening thing after another. Retold from the ballad. British Isles.

This Time, Tempe Wick, by Patricia Lee Gauch. Coward, McCann, 1974.
During the American Revolutionary War, a girl named Tempe Wick helped Washington's army as best she could. But hungry soldiers eventually mutinied, and tried to steal her horse. Tempe responded with cunning, then with force, to keep what was hers. Based on a legend from Jockey Hollow, New Jersey.

The Three Little Eggs, in *Black Fairy Tales* by Terrry Berger. Atheneum, 1969.
In this Swazi tale from South Africa, a woman takes her two children and leaves the husband who mistreats her. With the advice of magical eggs she finds, she defeats monsters and finds a new home.

The Three Spinners, in *More Tales from Grimm* by Wanda Gág. Coward, McCann, 1947, o.p.
An unskilled girl is forced to spin. Three old women offer magic help if she promises to invite them to her wedding. She does, and they explain their various deformities as the result of spinning. The groom forbids her to spin. Germany. There is also a Scandinavian version.

Two Old Women's Bet, in *Grandfather Tales* by Richard Chase. Houghton, 1948.
They bet on which one can make a bigger fool out of her husband. One convinces her spouse he is dead, the other makes hers a suit like "The Emperor's New Clothes." Appalachian.

Umai, in *The Inland Whale* by Theodora Kroeber. U. of California Press, c. 1959.
A Yurok legend in which the lake girl canoes to the ocean and meets the shining girl of the sunset. Native American.

Vasilisa and Prince Vladimir, in *Tales from atop a Russian Stove* by Janet Higonnet-Schnopper. Whitman, 1973, o.p.
Vasilisa, disguised as a man, wins her husband's freedom by beating the Prince's troops in wrestling and archery and the Prince in chess.

Wild Robin, retold by Susan Jeffers. Dutton, 1976.
Willful Robin gets a well-deserved scolding, runs away, and falls under the spell of the fairy people. A dream shows his sister Janet how to save Robin, and she does so. A "Tamlane" for younger children. British Isles.

Wiley, His Mama, and the Hairy Man, in *The People Could Fly: American Black Folktales* by Virginia Hamilton. Knopf, 1985.
A brave boy and his calm and tricky mama fool the Hairy Man three times.

Winter Rose, in *The Milky Way and Other Chinese Folk Tales* by Adet Lin. Harcourt, 1961, o.p.
Two sisters, searching for rose petals to cure their sick mother, fall into the clutches of a wizard, but trick him and escape with the roses.

The Wise Old Woman, in *The Sea of Gold and Other Tales from Japan* by Marianne Yamaguchi. Creative Arts, 1988.
The lord of a village orders all people over seventy-one killed, but a farmer hides his old mother and it is she who solves an invader's riddles and saves the village. The lord removes his edict.

The Wood Fairy, in *Favorite Fairy Tales Told in Czechoslovakia* by Virginia Haviland. Little, Brown, 1966, o.p.
A wood fairy entices a girl to dance and the girl's neglected work is done by magic.

The Young Head of the Family, in *The Fairy Ring* by Kate Douglas Wiggin. Doubleday, o.p.
A Chinese story of a girl who knows how to carry fire in paper (a lantern) and wind in paper (a fan). Her widowed father-in-law designates her head of the family and she leads it to prosperity. Different versions in *The Milky Way* by Adet Lin (Harcourt, o.p.), *With a Deep Sea Smile* by Virginia Tashjian (Little, 1974) and *Tales People Tell in China* by Robert Wyndham (o.p.). Not all have the head-of-family conclusion.

Goddesses

The Greek, Roman and Norse mythologies include many well-known stories about goddesses. Here are a few from other cultures.

The Buried Moon, in *More English Fairy Tales* by Joseph Jacobs. Dover, c. 1904. Also published separately in a retelling by Margaret Hodges. Little, Brown, 1990.
The moon rescues a man from the Evil Things in the Carland bog, but is herself captured. With the Wise Woman's guidance, the villagers rescue her.

The Fairy of Hawili Falls, in *Folk Tales from the Philippines* by Dorothy Lewis Robertson. Dodd, 1971, o.p.
The "fairy goddess" of the woods falls in love with a man who sees the beauty in nature.

The Living Kuan-Yin, in *Sweet and Sour: Tales from China* by Carol Kendall and Yao-wen Li. Houghton, c. 1979.
The goddess answers three questions for each pilgrim, but the generous Chin Po-wan promises three answers to those he meets along the way. How will he get an answer to his own question?

Song of Sedna, retold by Robert San Souci. Doubleday, 1981.
The legend of an Inuit woman becoming goddess of the sea.

Animal Tales

The Cock, the Mouse and the Little Red Hen, retold by Lorinda B. Cauley. Putnam, 1982.
The hen rescues her lazy housemates from the fox.

The Five Little Foxes and the Tiger, in *Animal Folktales around the World* by Kathleen Arnott. Walck, 1971, o.p.
Mrs. Fox saves herself and Mr. Fox from the tiger by using her wits, and brings her conceited husband down a peg at the same time. Bangladesh.

The Little Red Hen, retold by Margot Zemach. Farrar, 1983. Another version retold by Paul Galdone. Seabury, 1973. English/Spanish edition by Letty Williams. Prentice, 1969.
She will not share the bread with those who refused to help make it. England.

Nine-in-One Grr! Grr! A Folktale from the Hmong People of Laos, by Blia Xiong. Children's Book Press, 1989.
"That's terrible!" squawked Bird. "If Tiger has nine cubs each year, they will eat all of us!" What can Bird do to preserve nature's balance?

Two Donkeys, in *The Magic Orange Tree and Other Haitian Folktales* by Diane Wolkstein. Knopf, 1978.
Two donkeys change themselves into people for better treatment, but the jenny gets absorbed in housework and forgets to turn back.

The Wolf and the Seven Little Kids, in *Fairy Tales* by Jacob Grimm and Wilhelm Grimm. Various editions.
The mother goat saves her kids and kills the wolf.

This list was revised and annotated by Nancy Schimmel, but many others have contributed information: Camille Pronger, Marion Callery Morter, Dolly Larvick Barnes, Kendall Smith, Fran Stallings, Northern California Association of Children's Librarians—Social Concerns Committee, ALA-ALSC Discussion Group on Sexism in Library Materials for Children, University of Wisconsin School of Library and Information Studies Storytelling Class, Summer 1977 and 1981, University of California Graduate School of Library and Information Studies Storytelling Class, Summer 1979, UCLA Graduate School of Library and Information Science Storytelling Class, Summer 1982-4.

STORIES IN SERVICE TO PEACE

ONCE A SAMURAI WARRIOR WENT to a monastery and asked a monk, "Can you tell me about heaven and hell?" The monk answered, "I cannot tell you about heaven and hell. You are much too stupid." The warrior's face became contorted with rage. "Besides that," continued the monk, "you are very ugly." The warrior gave a scream and raised his sword to strike the monk. "That," said the monk unflinchingly, "is hell." The samurai slowly lowered his sword and bowed his head. "And that," said the monk, "is heaven."

This story from storyteller Ken Feit is included in an annotated list of Peace Stories available from Douglas R. Bland, 421 Guptil Avenue, Sumner, WA 98390.

When I was hired to tell stories at U.S. Army schools in Germany, and considered that I might have to cross through an anti-missile demonstration to get to a school (I didn't have to), I learned *The Wave*, another story from this list.

Storytellers for World Change puts out an occasional newsletter (subscriptions from John Porcino, 253 Long Plain Road, Amherst, MA 01002). Members have edited an anthology, *Spinning Tales— Weaving Hope: Stories of Peace, Justice and the Environment*, published in 1991 by New Society Publishers. Activities are included for each story.

Two more anthologies on the theme are *…And the Earth Lived Happily Ever After: Old and New Traditional Tales to Wage Peace*, edited by Floating Eaglefeather (Wages of Peace, 309 Trudeau Drive, Metairie, LA 70003) and *Peace Tales* by Margaret Read MacDonald (Linnet/Shoestring 1992).

Peace Stories

The Adventures of Charlie and His Wheat-Straw Hat: A Memorat Recounted by Berniece T. Hiser, by Mary Szilagyi. Putnam, 1986.
Charlie is so proud of the wheat-straw hat his grandmother makes him that he defies Confederate soldiers to keep it.

Brothers: A Hebrew Legend, retold by Florence B. Freedman. Harper, 1985.
Each brother thinks the other needs more of the harvest and tries to give it to him secretly.

The Cow-Tail Switch, in *The Cow-Tail Switch and Other West African Stories* by Harold Courlander and George Herzog. Holt, 1949.
A hunter fails to return from the hunt. Later, a son is born and asks where the father is. The older sons find his bones and reconstruct him. The father gives the cow-tail switch to the youngest, who asked for him, because a man is not truly dead as long as he is remembered.
The way I introduce or comment on a story can fit it into a peace program. I learned this story because I realized that the conclusion, that a man is not truly dead as long as he is remembered, is what would differentiate a nuclear war from all past wars. With no one left to remember us, we would all be truly dead.

The Fair Prince and His Brothers, in *Cap o' Rushes and other Folk Tales* by Winifred Finlay. Harvey, 1974, o.p.
The prince who will not fight, wins.

The Golden Earth, in *The Fire on the Mountain and Other Ethiopian Stories* by Harold Courlander and Wolf Lesau. Holt, 1950, o.p.
The Emperor, by a nice symbolic act, warns some European explorers that he does not intend to let his land be exploited by them.

The Grain Miracle, in *The Goddess Obscured: Transformation of the Grain Protectress from Goddess to Saint* by Pamela Berger. p.90. Beacon, 1985.
With the help of a farmer, Mary tricks Herod's soldiers on the flight into Egypt.

How the Beldys Stopped Fighting, in *Folktales of the Amur: Stories from the Russian Far East* by Dmitri Nagashkin. Harry N. Abrams, 1980, o.p.
Two wise and respected twins stop war by pretending to favor it but changing the rules to make it impossible.

I'm Tipingee, She's Tipingee, We're Tipingee Too, in *The Magic Orange Tree and Other Haitian Folktales* by Diane Wolkstein. Knopf, 1978.
Tipingee organizes her friends to wear red like her, so the old man who has come to take her away won't be able to pick her out.
On a level understandable to young children, this introduces the story of the non-violent resistance of the Danes to the Nazis during World War II. When the German invaders ordered all Jews to wear yellow stars, gentiles wore yellow stars also in protest, and helped most of the Jews escape the country.

The Laidly Worm of Spindlestone Heugh, in *English Fairy Tales* by Joseph Jacobs. Dover, 1967.
Childe Wind rescues his sister by kissing the dragon, not by slaying it.

The Lionmakers, from *The Panchatantra.* Translated by Arthur Ryder. U. Chicago Press, 1964.
The experts know how to do it but not when to stop. From a collection used for the education of princes in India, circa 500 CE. Another version is in *Just Enough to Make a Story*—that one is also on *Tell Me a Story: Nancy Schimmel* from Kartes Video. Still another version is "The Scholars and the Lion" in Harold Courlander's *The Tiger's Whisker* (o.p.) 7-adult.

Odilia and Aldaric, in *The Giant at the Ford And Other Legends of the Saints* by Ursula Synge. Atheneum, 1980, o.p. Also available on Milbre Burch's cassette, *Saints and Other Sinners* (Kind Crone).
A warrior rejects his blind daughter and she is raised in a convent. At baptism she regains her sight. Then begins a contest of wills between equally stubborn father and daughter. Alsace.

Once a Mouse, retold by Marcia Brown. Scribners, 1961.
Growing big and powerful often brings us to forget our humble past. India.

The People Who Hugged the Trees: An Environmental Folk Tale, adapted by Deborah Lee Rose. Roberts Rinehart, 1990.
Amrita loves the trees that protect her desert village from sandstorms. When a ruler orders the woods cut, she runs to hug her favorite tree and the other villagers do the same. The ruler is adamant until a sandstorm comes and he sees that the trees are more useful as trees than as a fort. India.

The Wave, adapted by Margaret Hodges from Lafcadio Hearn's *Gleaning in Buddha-fields.* Houghton, 1964.
An old man sets fire to his rice field to warn the village below of an approaching tidal wave.

This list was compiled by Nancy Schimmel and may be reproduced, in its entirety only, by any library, school, or peace organization. Please credit the source, *Just Enough to Make a Story,* and use recycled paper. Others who wish to reproduce the list, apply to Sisters' Choice.

ECOLOGY STORIES, SONGS AND SOURCES

Once there was a wise old man. He was so wise he could answer any question anyone ever asked him, no matter how difficult. One day, two young people were talking and they said, "We're going to fool that old man. We'll catch a bird, and go to the old man, and say, 'This that we hold in our hands today, is it alive or is it dead?' If he says 'Dead,' we'll turn it loose and let it fly, and if he says 'Alive,' we'll crush it."

So they caught a bird, and they carried it to that old man, and they said, "This that we hold in our hands today, is it alive or is it dead?" And that wise old man looked at those young people and he smiled. And he said, "It's in your hands."

Susan Griffin pointed this story out to me in a book of speeches by women. Fannie Lou Hamer had ended a speech with it at the NAACP Legal Defense Fund Institute in 1971. As I tell it around, people tell me that they have found it in other sources as well. Ms. Hamer was talking about "The Special Plight and the Role of Black Women," but the story can apply to any struggle, any choices people need to make. I have been using it in ecology programs, along with some of the following stories (approximate grade range indicated).

Some terrific true stories about kids helping solve environmental problems (drawing official attention to a toxic waste dump near their school, suggesting a solar solution to a city problem, planting trees) appear in *The Kid's Guide to Social Action: How to Solve the Social Problems You Choose—and Turn Creative Thinking into Positive Action* by Barbara A. Lewis (Free Spirit [400 First Avenue North, Suite 616, Minneapolis, MN 55401], 1991).

This list may be reprinted without permission by any non-profit educational or environmental group. Others apply to Sisters' Choice. Please give credit to *Just Enough to Make a Story* and PLEASE USE RECYCLED PAPER.

❖❖

Animalia, by Barbara Berger. Celestial Arts, 1982.
Brief tales of wise and holy people who have lived gently with animals. 3rd up.

Buffalo Gals and other Animal Presences, by Ursula LeGuin. ROC Fantasy, 1990. [c. 1987, Capra.]
Modern fantasy stories.

Come Again in the Spring, from *Richard Kennedy's Collected Stories*, illustrated by Marcia Sewell. Harper, 1987.
Old Hark refuses to go when Death comes in winter. The birds have stayed North because he feeds them and they will die if he goes. The birds help Hark in a wager with death. (Also published separately, o.p.) 3rd up.

Coyote at the Movies, by Tim McNulty in *Coyote's Journal*, edited by Steve Nemirow and others, illustrated by Harry Fonseca. Wingbow, 1982.
When he finds the lumber company promo film, Coyote knows just how to show it. Jr. high up.

The Crocodile in the Bedroom, from *Fables* by Arnold Lobel. Harper, 1980.
The Crocodile prefers the orderly flowers on his wallpaper to his wife's unruly garden. 1st up.

Crow Boy, by Taro Yashima. Viking, 1955.
Chibi is too shy to do well in school, but finally a sympathetic teacher helps him show what he learned walking over the mountains to school. 3rd up.

The Deer of Five Colors, in *The Magic Listening Cap: More Folk Tales from Japan* by Yoshiko Uchida. Creative Arts, 1987, c. 1955.
The deer hides in a remote forest fearing that men will kill him for his beautiful coat. A farmer he saves from drowning promises never to tell where he is, but when the ruler of the land dreams of the deer and offers a reward, the farmer forgets his promise. 2nd up.

Elijah's Violin, in *Elijah's Violin & Other Jewish Fairy Tales* by Howard Schwartz. Harper, 1983.
The youngest daughter asks her father to bring her Elijah's violin, which summons a prince when she plays it. Her jealous sisters drive him away, but she understands when the birds tell her the map she needs is on every leaf of their tree, and she rescues him. 3rd up.

Elsie Piddock Skips in her Sleep, from *Martin Pippin in the Daisy Field* by Eleanor Farjeon. Lippincott, o.p.
Elsie learns to skip rope from the fairies and years later, when she is an old woman, her special skill saves the town's precious land from development. Also in

A Storyteller's Choice, edited by Eileen Colwell. Walck, o.p. 3rd up.

Flossie and the Fox, by Patricia McKissack, illustrated by Rachel Isadora. Dial, 1986.
Flossie outfoxes the fox with a little lesson in animal identification. K-3rd.

The Golden Earth, in *Fire on the Mountain and Other Ethiopian Stories* by Harold Courlander and George Herzog. Holt, 1949, o.p.
The Emperor, by a nice symbolic act, warns some European explorers that he does not intend to let them exploit his land. 3rd up.

Her Seven Brothers, retold and illustrated by Paul Goble. Bradbury, 1988.
In this Cheyenne legend, a girl understands the speech of animals and birds. Her understanding leads her to her destiny as one of the eight stars in what we call the Big Dipper. "It is good to know that they once lived on earth. Listen to the stars! We are never alone at night." 3rd up.

Hidden Stories in Plants: Unusual and Easy-to-Tell Stories from Around the World Together with Creative Things to Do while Telling Them, by Anne Pellowski. Macmillan, 1990.

The Invisible Hunters/Los Cazadores Invisibles, by Harriet Rohmer, Octavio Chow, and Morris Vidaure, illustrated by Joe Sam. Children's Book Press, 1987.
The magical Dar plant makes the hunters invisible, but only so long as they do not use guns or sell the meat. When they get greedy, the magic turns against them. A story in English and Spanish from the Miskito people of Nicaragua. 1st-4th.

Justice, from *The Devil's Other Storybook* by Natalie Babbitt. Farrar, 1987.
A big-game hunter arrives in Hell and is ordered to hunt a rhinoceros using only a net, "...and it goes without saying that, without his gun, he was very much afraid he would find it." 3rd up.

Keepers of the Earth: Native American Stories and Environmental Activities for Children, by Michael J. Caduto and Joseph Bruchac. Fulcrum, 1988.
Separate teacher's guide has excellent background on Native American stories.

The Legend of the Bluebonnet, retold and illustrated by Tomie de Paola. Putnam, 1983.

In this retelling of a Native American tale, the elders learn that the drought is caused by people taking from the earth and not giving back. A young girl's unselfish gift brings rain, and the bluebonnet. K-3rd.

The Lion-Makers, from the *Panchatantra* translated by Arthur Ryder. U. of Chicago Press, 1964.
The experts know how to do it but not when to stop. Also on *Tell Me a Story: Nancy Schimmel* from Kartes Video and in *The Tiger's Whisker* by Harold Courlander and *Just Enough to Make a Story* (third edition) by Nancy Schimmel. 3rd up.

Miss Rumphius, by Barbara Cooney. Viking, 1982.
Great-aunt Alice was once a little girl who wanted to travel the world and then live by the sea, as her grandfather had. But there was one more thing she had to do. "What is that?" Alice asked her grandfather. "You must do something to make the world more beautiful," he told her. 1st-4th.

Mufaro's Beautiful Daughters, retold and illustrated by John Steptoe. Lothrop, 1987.
A snake is well treated by a young African woman who knows he is good for her garden. He turns out to be a handsome prince. 1st-4th.

Nine-in-One Grr! Grr! told by Blia Xiong, adapted by Cathy Spagnoli, illustrated by Nancy Hom. Children's Book Press, 1989.
"That's terrible!" squawked Bird. "If Tiger has nine cubs each year, they will eat all of us." What can Bird do to preserve nature's balance? K-3rd.

Ntombi's Song, by Jenny Seed, illustrated by Anno Berry. Beacon, 1989.
Ntombi, a Zulu six-year-old, overcomes her fear of the dark forest on her first trip to the store alone. K-3rd.

The People Who Hugged the Trees: An Environmental Folk Tale, adapted by Deborah Lee Rose, illustrated by Birgitta Saflund. Roberts Rinehart, 1990.
Amrita loves the trees that protect her desert village from sandstorms. When a ruler orders the woods cut, she runs to hug her favorite tree and the other villagers do the same. The ruler is adamant until a sandstorm comes and he sees that the trees are more useful as trees than as

a fort. Adapted from a story of Rajasthan, India. 1st-up.

The Rice-Puller of Chaohwa, in *The Tiger's Whisker and Other Tales from Asia and the Pacific* by Harold Courlander. Harcourt, 1959.
A farmer ruins his crop by impatience. China. K-up.

Salven mi Selva, by Monica Zak, illustrated by Bengt-Arne Runnerstrom. Sitesa, 1989.
The true story of Omar Castillo, who, when he was eight years old, convinced his father to walk with him from Mexico City to Tuxtla Gutiérrez to save Mexico's rain forest. Spanish only. (Available from Mariuccia Iaconi Book Imports, 1110 Mariposa St., San Francisco, CA.94107. English version forthcoming in 1992 from Volcano Press.) 1st-6th.

Skunk and Coyote, told by Johnny Moses on *Traditional Stories of the Northwest Coast.* Cassette from Red Cedar Circle, P.O.Box 1210, La Conner, WA 98257.
Skunk sent a strong message to Coyote, but it missed and settled on Tacoma, which has been smelly ever since.

Slower Than the Rest, from *Every Living Thing* by Cynthia Rylant. Bradbury, 1985.
Leo, who is "slower than the rest" in school and unhappy about being in a special class, wins recognition and pride for his report on forest fires, using his pet turtle as an example of an animal who couldn't escape. "It isn't fair for the slow ones," he concludes. 3rd-6th.

Song of the Trees, by Mildred D. Taylor, illustrated by Jerry Pinkney. Dial, 1975.
A black family in Mississippi during the Depression defend their forest from a white man who wants to cut it down and cheat them. This is a novella, not a short story, but terrific for reading aloud and could possibly be condensed for telling. 3rd-6th.

The Strange Folding Screen, in *Men from the Village Deep in the Mountains and other Japanese Folk Tales* compiled by Molly Bang, translated and illustrated by Garreth Bang. MacMillan, o.p.
A painted screen reminds a man of the frogs who persuaded him not to sell his land and thus saved the forest and pond.

The Tailor, in the introduction to *Just Enough to Make a Story* by Nancy Schimmel. Sisters' Choice, 1982. Also on *Plum Pudding: Stories and Songs with Nancy Schimmel and the Plum City Players.* Audio cassette or LP. Sisters' Choice, 1982.

As his coat wears out, the tailor makes a jacket from the unworn parts, then a vest, etc. "The Journey" from *Mouse Tales* by Arnold Lobel can be told with it for contrast. The mouse buys something new whenever anything breaks. "The Tailor" also appears, with activities, in *Spinning Tales—Weaving Hope: Stories of Peace, Justice and the Environment,* published in 1991 by New Society Publishers. 1st up.

The Tale of the Mandarin Ducks, retold by Katherine Paterson, illustrated by Leo and Diane Dillon. Dutton, 1990.

The lord orders the mandarin drake captured so he can admire its beauty, but the drake loses his lustre without his mate and his wild home. A kind maid turns the drake loose and is threatened with death, but the duck and drake return as people to save her. Japanese folktale. 1st up.

Talk, in *The Cow Tail Switch* by Harold Courlander and George Herzog. Holt, 1988, c. 1947. Also in *Best Loved Folktales of the World,* edited by Joanna Cole. Doubleday, 1982.

Inanimate objects start objecting to a man's treatment of them. 1st up.

Umai, in *The Inland Whale* by Theodora Kroeber. University of California Press, 1959. Also on *Plum Pudding.*

Umai waits and watches and catches the rhythm of the water before she proceeds on her canoe journey to the edge of the earth. 4th up.

Werburgh and the Troublesome Geese, in *The Giant at the Ford and Other Legends of the Saints* by Ursula Synge. Atheneum, 1980.

The convent's geese are harassing the nuns, destroying the garden, making a continual uproar. St. Werburgh finds that they are protesting being eaten, and forbids further slaughter (unless a goose is caught in the garden). Peace is restored, as is a goose already in a pie. 4th up.

Why Mosquitos Buzz in People's Ears: A West African Tale, retold by Verna Aardema. Dial, 1975.

The chain of responsibility for the owlet's death leads eventually to the mosquito.

Why the Sky Is Far Away: A Folktale from Nigeria retold by Mary-Joan Gerson. Harcourt, 1974.

Adapted from a story in *The Origin of Life and Death* by Ulli Beier.

Once the sky was close enough to touch and edible; but people wasted it, so it moved away.

The Wounded Wolf, by Jean Craighead George. Harper, 1978.

The pack feeds the wounded wolf until he can recover and hunt again. 1st up.

Ecology Songs

All God's Critters Got a Place in the Choir, words and music by Bill Staines, illustrated by Margot Zemach. Dutton, 1989.

A joyous celebration of all animal and human life. All ages.

All In This Together: 15 Ecology Songs for the Whole Family, composed by Nancy Schimmel, Candy Forest, and others. Sung by Candy Forest, Nancy Schimmel and The Singing Rainbows Youth Ensemble. Sisters' Choice Recordings SCR 467.

Parents' Choice Award-winning tape of songs about endangered species and habitats and the humane treatment of animals—in a variety of musical styles.

Dirt Made My Lunch, composed by Steve Van Zandt. Sung by Steve Van Zandt and the Banana Slug String Band.

BSSB 02. Available from Music for Little People.

The Banana Slugs have three tapes of silly but educational songs about plant parts, natural cycles, solar energy, etc.

Earthy Tunes: Nature Songs for Kids, ages 3-11 years. Sung by Mary Miché. Song Trek, 2600 Hillegass, Berkeley, CA 94704.

Essential songs, including "The Garden Song," "You Can't Make a Turtle Come Out."

Piggyback Planet, sung by Sally Rogers. RRR301. Available from Round River Records, 301 Jacob St., Seekonk, MA 02771.

Parents' Choice Award-winning tape of songs about ladybugs, recycling, etc., including one song in Spanish and a traditional Navaho song and Chinese song, both in English.

Plum Pudding: Stories and Songs with Nancy Schimmel and the Plum City Players. Sisters' Choice SCR365, tape or LP.

Several of the stories and songs relate to ecology: "The Tailor," "Umai," "A Place in the Choir," "The Witch Song."

Songwriting Together: Cooperative Songwriting to Build Closeness with the Earth and Each Other, by Sarah Pirtle. Available from Sarah Pirtle, 54 Thayer Road, Greenfield, MA 01301.

Audio cassette of 22 songs including "The Mahogany Tree" about the rainforest and "Thinking Like a Mountain," with 17 song patterns for children to create their own songs. Includes a teacher's guide, lyrics, guitar chords, and complete lesson plans for songwriting in small cooperative groups using a whole language approach.

Spin, Spider, Spin, composed and sung by Marcia Berman and Patty Zeitlin. Educational Activities AR 551.

Friendly songs about snakes, bugs, etc.

SISTERS' CHOICES

HERE ARE SOME STORIES WE have told, with sources, additional comments, and *approximate* age range.

Barney McCabe, in *Ain't You Got a Right to the Tree of Life? The People of Johns Island, South Carolina—Their Faces, Their Words, and Their Songs* by Guy and Candie Carawan. Revised and expanded edition U. Georgia Press, 1989. Also told by Mrs. Janie Hunter on *Moving Star Hall Singers*, Folkways PS 3841.

Jack and Mary get in trouble with the witch. When she starts cutting down the tree they hid in, they call their dogs to rescue them. This story is related to an African story, "Tsimbarumé the Hardened Bachelor," retold by Hugh Tracey in *The Lion on the Path* (London, Routledge and Kegan Paul, 1967). Tsimbarumé, a hunter, follows a young woman down a hole into another world where she is held captive by a witch. The witch tricks Tsimbarumé into a tree, then starts to chop down the tree with her tooth. The hunter calls his dogs with a magic song. The dogs attack the witch, but she kills them with her tooth. He calls them again, and the song is so powerful that it brings the dogs to life again and they kill the witch.

I learned "Barney McCabe" from Guy Carawan, who learned it from Mrs. Janie Hunter. I do it *a capella*, as she does, but I teach Jack and Mary's song to most of the audience and Barney McCabe's to the back row before I start. I tell it in my own words rather than trying to reproduce the regional speech. After I tell this story, I usually talk about how stories travel around. Sometimes I sing Bonnie Lockhart's "Witch Song" (*Plum Pudding*, Sisters' Choice Recordings, 1982) which presents a positive view of witches as herbal healers, midwives and storytellers. Or else I just talk about how Jack in the story seems to be a know-it-all big brother but he isn't (they are twins), but sometimes boys act that way, so is it any wonder some girls grow up to be witches. 6-10, adult.

The Basket, in *Patterns of Renewal* by Laurens Van der Post. p. 4-5. Pendle Hill Pamphlet, number 121. Pendle Hill Publications (Wallingford, PA 19086), 1962. This African story of a man who breaks a promise to his sky-born wife is a commentary on marriage, cross-cultural understanding, or what you will. 12-adult.

The Bear Says North, in *The Shepherd's Nosegay* by Parker Fillmore. Harcourt, 1920, o.p.
A good short one from Finland in which fox tricks bear. Your listeners have to be watchers too. 6-12.

Brer Rabbit's Human Weakness, in *Terrapin's Pot of Sense* by Harold Courlander. Holt, 1957, o.p.
As the animal-camp-meeting preachers take a break, Brer Rabbit persuades them all to confess their "human weakness," then confesses that his weakness is gossip. 8-adult.

Bye-Bye, in *The Magic Orange Tree and Other Haitian Folktales* by Diane Wolkstein. Knopf, 1978.
In this Haitian folktale, the birds try to carry Turtle to New York, but he can't keep his mouth shut. All ages.

Caps for Sale, retold by Esphyr Slobodkina. Harper, 1947. Scholastic pbk, 1976.
Monkeys imitate peddler, audience imitates teller for almost automatic participation story. Russian. 3-6.

The Cat on the Dovrefell, in *East of the Sun and West of the Moon* by P. C. Asbjornsen, translated by George Dasent. Dover, o.p.
An unsentimental Christmas story, from Norway, with trolls. 5-11.

Clever Manka, in *Womenfolk and Fairy Tales* compiled by Rosemary Minard. Houghton, 1975.
Also in *The Shepherd's Nosegay, Time for Fairy Tales, Fools and Funny Fellows* (all o.p.) and on *Tell Me a Story: Nancy Schimmel.*

A shepherd's daughter solves the burgomaster's riddles, marries him, disobeys his order not to show herself more clever than he, and outwits him again in order to keep him. Czechoslovakian. 10-adult.

The Cow-Tail Switch, in *The Cow-Tail Switch and Other West African Stories* by Harold Courlander and George Herzog. Holt, 1949.
A hunter fails to return from the hunt. Later, a son is born and asks where his father is. The older sons find his bones and reconstruct him. The father gives the cow-tail switch to the youngest, who asked for him, because a man is not truly dead as long as he is remembered. 8-adult.

Coyote at the Movies, by Tim McNulty in *Coyote's Journal* edited by Steven Nemirow. Wingbow, 1982.
When he finds the lumber company promo film, Coyote knows just how to show it. Junior high-adult.

Drum, from *Elderberry Flute Song* by Peter Blue Cloud. Crossings, 1982, o.p.
Badger's son and Coyote in a teaching story about not teaching. Adult.

Elijah's Violin, in *Elijah's Violin & Other Jewish Fairy Tales* by Howard Schwartz. Harper, 1983.
The youngest daughter asks her father to bring her Elijah's violin, which summons a prince when she plays it. Her jealous sisters drive the prince away, but with the help of the wise woman, she rescues him. 8-adult.

The Fairy Frog, in *Black Fairy Tales* by Terry Berger. Macmillan, 1974.
Tombi-Ende is buried alive by her jealous sisters, but she keeps crying out, "I am Tombi-Ende, I am not dead, I am alive like one of you," and an enchanted frog hears her and saves her. Swazi. 7-10.

The Fat Cat, a Danish Folktale retold by Jack Kent. Scholastic, 1972.
The Danish variant of the common folktale in which one character eats all the

others. Works well as a dramatized story with an audience that includes pre-schoolers and older children or pre-schoolers and adults. As a picture book, 4–7.

Fiddler, Play Fast, Play Faster, in *The Long Christmas* by Ruth Sawyer. Viking, 1941, o.p.
A fairly shivery Christmas story in which a fiddler bests the devil. Based on a legend from the Isle of Man. 11-Adult.

The Foolish Frog, on *Birds, Beasts, Bugs and Bigger Fishes.* Pete Seeger. Folkways FC 7011. *The Foolish Frog* was also published as a book by Macmillan, o.p.
I introduce this *cante fable* about the big party down at the corner store by saying it's a story about the olden times when daddies didn't know how to cook supper, or claimed they didn't, so they never had to worry about getting all the food ready and hot at the same time. Consequently, they never understood how important it was for the eaters to be there when supper was ready. Good for mixed-age audiences, all children or children and adults.

The Freedom Bird, in *Joining In* by Teresa Miller. Yellow Moon, 1988.
All ages.
The hunter tries to demolish the obstreperous bird, but the bird keeps singing nyaa! nyaa! and so does the audience.

The Golden Earth, in *The Fire on the Mountain and Other Ethiopian Stories* by Harold Courlander and Wolf Lesau. Holt, 1950, o.p.
By a symbolic act, the Emperor warns some European explorers that he does not intend to let his land be exploited by them. 9-adult.

The Grain Miracle, in *The Goddess Obscured: Transformation of the Grain Protectress from Goddess to Saint* by Pamela Berger, p.90. Beacon, 1985.
With the help of a farmer, Mary tricks Herod's soldiers on the flight into Egypt. 10-adult.

The Handsome Prince, in *Just Enough to Make a Story* by Nancy Schimmel. Sisters' Choice, 1991. Also on *Tell Me A Story: Nancy Schimmel,* produced by Kartes Videocommunications and available from Sisters' Choice.
The "sleeping beauty" does not want to be kissed. The prince insists, to his regret. All ages.

The House in the Woods, in *Once in the First Times: Folk Tales from the Philippines* by Elizabeth Hough Sechrist. MacRae Smith, 1969, o.p.
A Hansel and Gretel variant with no stepmother and no witch! 6-adult.

The Huckabuck Family and How They Raised Pop Corn in Nebraska and Quit and Came Back, in *Rootabaga Stories* by Carl Sandburg. Harcourt, 1922.
Pony Pony Huckabuck stars in a Thanksgiving tall tale that isn't oppressively thankful. 6–9.

I'm Tipingee, She's Tipingee, We're Tipingee Too, in *The Magic Orange Tree and Other Haitian Folktales* by Diane Wolkstein. Knopf, 1978.
Tipingee organizes her friends to wear red like her, so the old man who has come to take her away won't be able to pick her out. I tell this as I saw Diane tell it, asking individual girls to wear red to help Tipingee to trick the old man. Since this is yet another bad stepmother story, I generally follow it with "The Lion's Whisker." Good for mixed-age audiences.

Indian Saynday and White Man Saynday, in *Winter-Telling Stories* by Alice Marriott. Crowell, 1947.
The Native American trickster proves trickier than his white counterpart. Kiowa. 6–13.

In the Beginning, in *Raven-Who-Sets-Things-Right: Indian Tales of the Northwest Coast* by Fran Martin. Harper, 1975, o.p.
Raven as trickster exploits the soporific qualities of storytelling to steal water from the one who is hoarding it. Good for tandem telling. 5-adult.

It Could Always Be Worse retold by Margot Zemach. Farrar, Straus, 1977.
My mother used to tell me this story about a man whose house was too small, so I don't follow the book closely, but I do keep it kosher—no pigs. It's fun to do as an audience participation story with groups of children being the family and animals. Pre-school–7 and mixed ages.

The Journey, in *Mouse Tales* by Arnold Lobel. Harper, 1972.
As each new purchase wears out, the mouse buys a replacement, including a new pair of feet. 4–7.

King o' the Cats, in *More English Fairy Tales* by Joseph Jacobs. Dover, 1967.
The sexton sees a funeral procession of cats, but the real surprise comes when he tells his wife about it. I introduce this mildly spooky story by saying, "This is a story from the old times when the graveyard was right next to the church, so the sexton, who takes care of the church, also dug the graves." That takes care of *sexton* without sounding quite like a definition. 7-adult.

The Laidly Worm of Spindlestone Heugh, in *English Fairy Tales* by Joseph Jacobs. Dover, 1967.
Childe Wind rescues his sister by kissing the dragon, not by slaying it. Jacobs retold this from a ballad whose tune has been lost. I found that the tune of "The Cottage Door" in *Folk Songs of Peggy Seeger* (o.p.) fits the meter and mood of Lady Margaret's verses in this story exactly, so I sing them to that tune. 10-adult.

Lazy Jack, in *English Fairy Tales* by Joseph Jacobs. Dover, 1967.
Jack takes his mother's advice literally, which doesn't work, but leads him to win a bag of gold. I don't like the idea of the girl's father handing her over to Jack as a reward, so I have Jack court her first. Gives her time to grow up, too—"girls" are too young to get married. 4-10.

The Lion on the Path, in *The Story Vine* by Anne Pellowski. Macmillan, 1984.
A farmer entrances a threatening lion with his thumb-piano, but is stuck until Rabbit helps him escape. I prefer Anne Pellowski's version, without the disparaging remark about women that's in the version in *The Lion in the Path* by Hugh Tracey. (Routledge and Kegan Paul, London, 1967.) 5–adult.

The Lionmakers, from *The Panchatantra,* translated by Arthur Ryder. U. Chicago Press, 1964.
The experts know how to do it but not when to stop. From a collection used for the education of princes in India, circa 500 CE. Another version is in *Just Enough to Make a Story*—that one is also on *Tell Me a Story: Nancy Schimmel* from Kartes Video. Still another version is "The Scholars and the Lion" in Harold Courlander's *The Tiger's Whisker* (o.p.) 7-adult.

The Lion's Whiskers, in *The Lion's Whiskers, Tales of High Africa* by Brent Ashabranner and Russell Davis. Little, Brown, 1959, o.p.
A woman tames a lion in order to win the love of her little stepson. An antidote to all

those bad-stepmother stories and a hint about why they exist. 7-adult.

The Little Red Hen, retold by Margot Zemach. Farrar, 1983.
The hen will not share the bread with those who refused to help make it. I learned this story from my mother. There are many versions. Zemach's, like my mother's, doesn't say anything about the hen sharing the bread with her chicks. English. 4-6.

The Magic Wings: A Tale from China retold by Diane Wolkstein. Dutton, 1983
The goose girl is determined to grow wings, and after all the women in the country become involved, she does. Also in *Joining In*, compiled by Teresa Miller (Yellow Moon, 1988) with instructions from Diane on doing it as a participation story. Diane's version of an old Chinese tale (found as "Growing Wings" in Adet Lin's *The Milky Way*) is the one I prefer to tell, as Diane's goose girl is not wimpy. I tell it as Diane does, getting four children up front flapping their arms, and flying the goose girl at the end (see photo on back cover). 5-7 and mixed ages.

The Man Who Walked on Water, in *Tales of the Dervishes* by Idries Shah. Dutton, 1970.
The young man who earnestly, but incorrectly, recites the text gets results anyway. After one of my students told this story about how it's okay to make mistakes, she immediately said, "I made a mistake—I forgot to say that reciting the text would bring you to such a high state of enlightenment *that you could walk on water.*" The class reaction was that the story was much better her way—just knowing that the text can produce a high state of enlightenment, but not knowing about walking on water till the very end. So it really *is* okay to make mistakes. (However, I think it would be a mistake to announce the title of the story before you told it.) Adult.

Mr. Fox, in *English Fairy Tales* by Joseph Jacobs. Dover, 1967.
Lady Mary investigates the castle of her fiancé and finds him to be a Bluebeard; her brothers and friends destroy him. 12-adult.

The Mitten, an Old Ukrainian Folktale retold by Alvin Tresselt. Lothrop, 1964.
A succession of increasingly large animals crowd into a mitten to keep warm. A tiny cricket is the last straw. I tell the core of this story using the string trick for "The Yam Thief." The loop taken off the thumb is the hole formed as the seam begins to give, into which the cricket puts her head, causing the whole seam to go. A teacher pointed out to me that if the thing has fingers, it is a glove, not a mitten. Fiddlesticks. 3-7.

Mujina, in *Kwaidan: Stories and Studies of Strange Things* by Lafcadio Hearn. C. E. Tuttle, 1971.
In this chilling Japanese tale, a man flees a ghost only to find that the person he takes refuge with is just as ghostly. 12-adult.

Nine-in-One Grr! Grr! A Folktale from the Hmong People of Laos retold by Blia Xiong. Children's Book Press, 1989.
"That's terrible!" squawked Bird. "If Tiger has nine cubs each year, they will eat all of us!" What can Bird do to preserve nature's balance? 4-8.

The Old Woman and Her Pig, in *The Old Woman and Her Pig and Ten Other Stories* by Anne Rockwell. Harper, 1979.
The old woman asks everyone for help getting her pig over the stile but only the cat will bargain with her. This cumulative tale can be made into a participation story by coaching the front row of listeners to say "No!" as you ask each in turn for help (until you get to the designated cat). The shy ones can just shake their heads, and of course you can always take silence as a refusal. For telling solo, remember to start fairly slowly if you want to speed up on the return trip. English. Pre-school.

Owl, in *The Magic Orange Tree and Other Haitian Folktales* by Diane Wolkstein. Knopf, 1978.
Owl thinks he is ugly, and is afraid to visit his girlfriend by daylight. I like to tell this *cante fable* in junior highs and middle schools. 10-adult.

The Pancake, in *Just Enough to Make a Story* by Nancy Schimmel. Sisters' Choice, 1991.
The pancake leaps from the pan and evades all pursuers until he meets the pig. Similar to "The Gingerbread Boy" and "The Bun." Norwegian. Pre-school. As a tandem story, pre-school-8.

The Pangs of Ulster, from the *Táin Bó Cuailnge,* translated by Thomas Kinsella. Oxford U. Press, 1970.
A woman in labor races on foot against the king's chariot and delivers twins on the finish line. Adult.

Patches, in *Men from the Village Deep in the Mountains* by Garret Bang. Macmillan, 1973 o.p.
This Japanese tale of an actor mistaken for Badger, the shape-changing trickster of Japanese folklore, has a most satisfying ending. When I tell "Patches," I often sing "Sho-joji" first. It's also from Japan and also about badgers. On *Berman/Barlin: Dance–a–Story, Sing–a–Song*, B/B Records, 570 N. Arden Blvd., Los Angeles, CA 90004. "The Silver on the Hearth" goes well in the same set as it also ends with snakes producing money. 8-adult.

The Pedlar of Swaffham, in *More English Fairy Tales* by Joseph Jacobs. Dover, 1967.
A peddler heeds the message in his dream and finds a treasure. There's a Jewish version in *Souls on Fire: Portraits and Legends of the Hasidic Masters* (o.p.) by Elie Wiesel. 9-adult.

A Penny a Look, An Old Story Retold by Harve Zemach. Farrar, 1971.
Harve Zemach took a Japanese tale of a schemer caught in his own scheme and made it the story of a rascal and his lazy brother, in a European setting. The Folktellers changed the brothers to sisters and moved them to the American South, which is the way Gay Ducey tells it, and I picked it up from her. The Folktellers do it as a tandem story. 7-adult.

Persephone and Demeter, in *The Road to Eleusis* by Robert Gordon Wasson. Harcourt, 1978.
I was inspired for the first time to tell a Greek myth by Jean Shinoda Bolen's *Goddesses in Everywoman: A New Psychology of Women* (Harper, 1984). I found a translation I liked of the Homeric hymn to Demeter in Wasson's book, from which I have taken phrases and the general structure of the story. The sequel I tell, "Persephone in Love," I elaborated from a paragraph on page 199 of *Goddesses in Everywoman*. I also usually tell "The Apple of Discord" after that, using the brief retelling on page 263 of *Goddesses*. 11-adult.

Petronella by Jay Williams, in *Don't Bet on the Prince: Contemporary Feminist Fairy Tales in North America and England* by Jack Zipes. Routledge, 1986. Also in Jay Williams' *The Practical Princess and*

Other Liberating Fairy Tales (o.p.) and published separately as a picture book (o.p.).

The third child of a royal couple performs the enchanter's three difficult tasks to rescue a prince, then she has second thoughts about him. 9–adult.

The Rice-Puller of Chaohwa, in *The Tiger's Whisker and Other Tales from Asia and the Pacific* by Harold Courlander. Harcourt, 1959, o.p.

A farmer ruins his crop by impatience. A librarian told me of a parent wanting teaching materials because his child was having trouble learning to print lower case. The child's age? Two and a half. I learned this story to tell at her library. 2 1/2 to adult.

The Riddles, in *World Tales* by Idries Shah. Harcourt, 1979, o.p. for all practical purposes (a costly edition is available from Johnson Reproductions/ Harcourt).

The self-assured daughter of a wood-gatherer saves the kingdom by answering a demon's riddles. Two of the riddles also appear in "Clever Manka." Turkestan. 9–adult.

Señor Coyote and the Dogs, in *Ride with the Sun: An Anthology of Folk Tales and Stories from the United Nations* by Harold Courlander. McGraw-Hill, 1955, o.p.

Coyote outruns the dogs, but when he criticizes his own tail, he gets himself in trouble again. 6–adult.

The Silver on the Hearth, in *Ride with the Sun: An Anthology of Folk Tales and Stories from the United Nations* by Harold Courlander. McGraw-Hill, 1955, o.p.

A poor farmer prays for riches "here on my own hearth" and finds a jar of silver in his field. Thinking it can't be his, he leaves it. His wife tells a neighbor, who digs up the jar and finds it full of snakes. So he empties it down the farmer's chimney, where the snakes turn to silver again, on the farmer's hearth. Afghanistan. 10–adult.

The Skull, in *The Book of Ghosts and Goblins* by Ruth Manning-Sanders. Dutton, 1973, o.p.

An orphan girl de-haunts and wins a castle by defending a skull from the skeleton that wants to steal it. I prefer to leave the little girl with the castle, playmates and servants she has won from the skeleton. She doesn't need—and the story doesn't need—the promise of a prince later. Tyrolian. 8–11.

Strawberries, in *Homespun: Tales from America's Favorite Storytellers* by Jimmy Neil Smith. Crown, 1988.

The first man and woman quarrel, and she leaves. A spirit creates the strawberry to remind her of her love for her husband. A Cherokee legend retold by Gayle Ross. 10–adult.

The Three Billy Goats Gruff, retold by Marcia Brown. Harcourt, 1957.

Goats trick troll, smash same. Norwegian. 3–7.

Ticoumba and the President, in *The Piece of Fire and Other Haitian Tales* by Harold Courlander. Harcourt, 1964, o.p.

Uppity citizen twists president's words to avoid punishments. This trickster tale has one of the riddles used in "Clever Manka" but an entirely different mood. A good story for two tellers. 10-13, adult.

The Tiger's Minister of State, in *The Tiger's Whisker, and Other Tales from Asia and the Pacific* by Harold Courlander. Harcourt, 1959, o.p.

The rabbit saves his neck by showing that in affairs of state, one is better off without a sense of smell. Burma. 6–adult.

Two Donkeys, in *The Magic Orange Tree and Other Haitian Folktales* by Diane Wolkstein. Knopf, 1978.

Two donkeys change themselves into people for better treatment, but the jenny forgets to turn back. Funniest moral I've found. 5–adult.

Two Pickpockets, in *Favorite Folktales from Around the World* by Jane Yolen. Pantheon, 1986.

A short, touching and funny story of two pickpockets who marry and plan to raise a family of pickpockets. England. 12–adult.

Umai, in *The Inland Whale* by Theodora Kroeber. U. of California Press, c. 1959.

A Yurok legend in which the lake girl canoes to the ocean and meets the shining girl of the sunset. Native American. 10–adult.

Wait Till Martin Comes, in *The Ghost and I, Scary Stories for Participatory Telling* by Jennifer Justice. Yellow Moon, 1992 [forthcoming].

A kitten, a cat, a bobcat and a mountain lion terrify a lost traveller, then leave. A ghost-story spoof, good for telling after a scary one. 8–11.

The Wave, adapted by Margaret Hodges from Lafcadio Hearn's *Gleaning in Buddha-fields*. Houghton, 1964.

An old man sets fire to his rice field to warn the village below of an approaching tidal wave. 9–adult.

Where the Wild Things Are, by Maurice Sendak. Harper, 1963.

Max gets wild, dinner arrives anyway. I would never have had the chuzpah to do Sendak without the illustrations if I hadn't seen the Folktellers do it. They have the audience put on their wolf suits first, and practice roaring their terrible roars, etc. The audience warms up during the story's description of the wild things, and lets loose for the wild rumpus—thus taking care of all those pages without text. 3–7.

Who Can Break a Bad Habit, in *African Wonder Tales* by Frances Carpenter. Doubleday, o.p.

The rabbit and monkey bet on who can break a habit. This story amuses young children and, for older children and adults, comments on the use of gesture in storytelling. A good one for two tellers.

The Woodcutter's Story by Nancy Schimmel, on *Plum Pudding: Stories and songs with Nancy Schimmel and the Plum City Players.* Nancy Schimmel. LP or audio cassette. Sisters' Choice, 1982. Also in print in *Best-Loved Stories Told at the National Storytelling Festival*, compiled, edited and published by the National Association for the Preservation and Perpetuation of Storytelling, 1991.

The youngest prince gets where he needs to go by letting himself be sidetracked from his princely role. 10–adult.

The Yam Thief, in *Strings on Your Fingers: How to Make String Figures* by Harry and Elizabeth Helfman. Morrow, 1965, o.p.

A string story in which the thief gets away with the yams. From the islands of the Torres Strait. All ages.

Title Index

Sources for stories referred to in the text but not listed here will be found in Sisters' Choices. Titles in italics are books, records, films or periodicals; others are stories or songs. Bold face numbers indicate information on sources.

Subject Index

Bold face numbers indicate information on sources.

SISTERS' CHOICE
RECORDINGS AND BOOKS

RECORDINGS

Plum Pudding: Stories and Songs with Nancy Schimmel and the Plum City Players
    SCR 365 (LP) **$5.00**
    SCR 365 (Cassette).................................. **$11.50**
Traditional and original stories and songs for school-age children and adults.
Stories: Umai, The Woodcutter's Story, The Tailor.
Songs: The Witch Song, Little Sure Shot, Al Tambor (in Spanish), A Place in the Choir.

Tell Me a Story: Nancy Schimmel........... **$15.00**
30 minute "live" videotape of traditional and original stories for school-age children and adults.
Stories: The Lionmakers, Clever Manka, The Pedlar of Swaffham, The Handsome Prince (origami story).

Dinosaur and Other Songs from Plum City
    PCR 101 (Cassette) **$9.00**
Original songs for pre-school and primary kids by Nancy Schimmel, Bonnie Lockhart and Ann Hershey, includes Tell Me a Story, The Tortoise and the Hare, Halloween Makes Me Scared and Kids' Boogie.

All In This Together: 15 Ecology Songs for the Whole Family
    SCR 467 (Cassette)................................... **$11.50**
Parent's Choice award-winning tape of songs about animals and trees sung by Candy Forest, Nancy Schimmel, Laurie Lewis and The Singing Rainbows Youth Ensemble. Intended for school-age kids, but three-year-olds love My Sister's a Whale in the Sea and I'm a Reptile. A songbook with study guide is in preparation.

Head First and Belly Down
    SCR 468 (Cassette) Spring 1992 .... **$11.50**
More ecology songs sung by The Singing Rainbows, Candy Forest and Laurie Lewis about otters and other critters, recycling, solar energy and more. Includes Somos el Barco sung in Spanish, and songs by Nancy Schimmel, Candy Forest, and Malvina Reynolds. Songbook with study guide to come.

Magical Songs
    CR040 T (Cassette) **$11.50**
Songs for the middle young written and sung by Malvina Reynolds with a children's chorus. Includes Don't Push Me and Lambeth Children.

Artichokes, Griddlecakes and Other Good Things
    Pacific Cascade LPC 7018 (Cassette) **$11.50**
Malvina sings intelligent songs for younger kids, including Eight Candles, I Live in a City, and În Bethlehem.

Funnybugs, Giggleworms and Other Good Friends
    Pacific Cascade LPC 7025 (Cassette) **$11.50**
Malvina sings her animal songs, assisted by the children's favorite, Nancy Raven. Includes Rabbits Dance, You Can't Make a Turtle Come Out, Hello Ladybug.

SONGBOOK

Tweedles and Foodles for Young Noodles by Malvina Reynolds **$5.75**
14 Malvina Reynolds songs "all full of dance-around" for preschool through primary age kids, with guitar chords and easy but interesting piano arrangements. Illustrated by Jody Robbin. Includes Rabbits Dance, I Live in a City.

Please include sales tax if you are a California resident, and 10% of price for US postage and handling. Discounts available for quantity orders. Sisters' Choice, 1450 Sixth Street, Berkeley, CA 94710. (510) 524-5804.